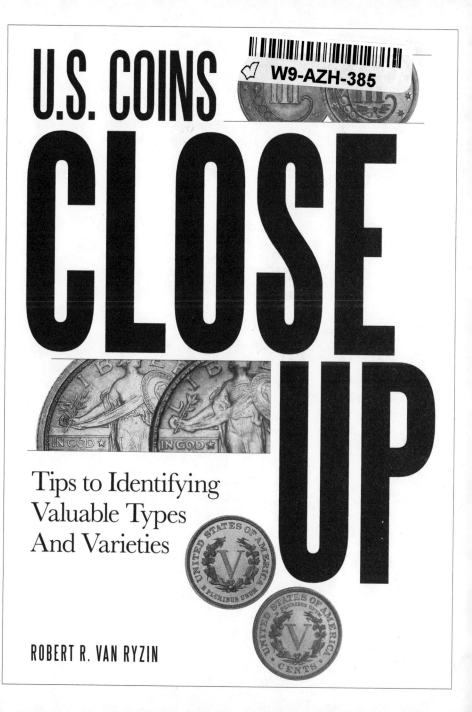

U.S. COINS
CLOSE
UP

W9-AZH-385

Tips to Identifying
Valuable Types
And Varieties

ROBERT R. VAN RYZIN

Published by

Krause Publications, a division of F+W Media, Inc.
700 East State Street • Iola, WI 54990-0001
715-445-2214 • 888-457-2873
www.krausebooks.com

To order books or other products call toll-free 1-800-258-0929
or visit us online at www.shopnumismaster.com

ISBN-13: 978-1-4402-2982-4
ISBN-10: 1-4402-2982-1

Cover Design by Jana Tappa
Designed by Jana Tappa
Edited by Caitlin Spaulding

Printed in USA

Table of Contents

Acknowledgements

When I began collecting coins in the mid-1970s, one of the first things I did was to join a local coin club. There, I not only learned more about the hobby but I also established some friendships that have lasted a lifetime. One of those I met through the local club was its then-president, Randy Miller. Randy's passion for the hobby and his knowledge was readily evident. This has proven itself in the years since, as he makes a living as a professional numismatist, operating Chief Coin & Supply, LLC, Oshkosh, Wis.

Recently, Randy allowed me access to his extensive inventory in the preparation of close-up images for this book. These included some very rare coins that he let me handle and place under a digital microscope. Without his cooperation, much of what you'll see within could not have come to fruition, and if it did, it would certainly be of lesser quality. I greatly appreciate and thank him for his efforts in this regard, the knowledge he imparted in preparation of the images and other aspects of this book, and his friendship and support through the years.

I also want to thank Alan Herbert for his contribution of the Foreword for this book. Alan is a renowned error and variety specialist and the author of several important books in the field, including Warman's U.S. Coin Collecting. Even if you've never read one of his books, if you've opened a copy of any Krause Publications periodical, you've likely read something he has written. Known as the "Answer Man," Alan has been fielding readers' questions on coins, medals, tokens and paper money for many years. I am grateful such a well-known hobby figure like Alan agreed to contribute to this book.

— Robert R. Van Ryzin

Foreword

For every 1,000 collectors, there are one or two whose interest lies more in the historical value than the monetary value, allowing curiosity to guide their collecting feet. A standout among that tiny minority is the author of this book, who digs into the nooks and crannies of coin collecting for the most interesting tidbits of information. His favorite pastime is leading his readers on an educational journey – one that is not boring or annoying.

The veteran collector may pass this by, certain that he or she "knows it all," and doesn't need a book to add to their store of knowledge. Frankly, I would be amazed if you could read it cover to cover and come away saying, "I didn't see one single thing I didn't know." I'd put good money on the line that you couldn't honestly say that.

Putting it bluntly, this book is crammed with facts, well-illustrated and specifically prepared for both the novice and experienced collector. Adding to the mix are explanations – definitions if you will – that allow the reader to easily understand the "why" behind our coin designs. Bob approaches coins with the eye and mind of the journalist, asking why, where, when, how and what.

This approach makes for easy reading.

It's refreshing to allow someone else to do the lengthy research needed to answer the recurring questions. Now that you've turned the first few pages, it's time to find your comfortable chair where you and this "easy read" can curl up, because once started, you may read straight through to the back cover. It will be an important addition to your coin reference library – or the start of a library.

Congratulations on another fine book.

— Alan Herbert
Author
Warman's U.S. Coin Collecting

Introduction

One of the undeniable joys of collecting, whether it be antique furniture, art glass, modern art, comics, movie posters, stamps or, in this case, money, is the thrill of the hunt. It often seems more important and exhilarating than the actual possession of the item that was so fervently and diligently sought.

You can find yourself looking through catalog after catalog of auction lots, examining specimen after specimen, to find that one special item – the one that in many ways "completes" your collection and is, in fact, that special piece few others can possess or have the wisdom to do so. This is what ties all collectors together: the common pursuit of the seemingly unobtainable that, once obtained, justifies the collector's existence, the long hours of pursuit, the looks of non-comprehension from non-collectors, including spouses, who sometimes question the outlay of funds to acquire that special collectible.

I, for example, especially enjoy the hunt. It sometimes consumes me. It sometimes makes me raise my bid higher than my preset limit to acquire an object of my desire. It makes me spend money on items that sometimes, frankly, I should have avoided. But when caught up in the hunt, there's nothing that can keep me from going after that seemingly life-affirming collectible that has presented itself to me.

If I've learned one thing bidding in auctions and buying collectibles in general, it is that it's easy to talk yourself into anything. Perhaps this little mark on a coin or medal isn't that bad. Or, worse yet, this item has to be rare since I haven't seen it before, or because estimates are that this many or that many exist, or that this many or that many are the only ones graded this high. Plus, there's the inevitable: I may never get another chance to obtain this collectible. So if you are just entering the hobby, you'll soon learn as I did, that you have to gain as much knowledge of what you're buying or attempting to buy as you can in order to protect yourself from making a bad decision.

For instance, just knowing how many of a given item were minted or how many were released to the public isn't always good enough. There may have been more melted or worn, hoarded or exported than another date and mint of the same denomination. Changes in a design during a given year could have led to a rare type or a scarce mintmarked issue. Also, minting processes at this or that mint might have caused an issue to be only encountered fully struck on a scarce number of pieces.

Out of necessity, you have to become an expert. In doing so, you learn there is no better teacher than study and studying the topic close up. To do so, you will need not only good sources of information, such as books and periodicals, but also an understanding of the minting process. One of the best ways to begin to do this is to grab a magnifying glass and dive right in. With a good glass, you'll quickly discover the difference between lines on the surface of a coin added during the minting process and those produced after a coin left the mint, either by damage or artificial means. You'll also learn to spot wear and to distinguish it from strike weakness.

I've always found it fun to look at coins under high magnification. I like seeing signs of metal flow from the original striking and examining details such as mintmarks and their styles close up. There are those in the hobby who say a low power magnifying glass is a collector's best friend. I like a high power, 10x minimum glass to explore a coin, medal or token. My recommendation is to try both, but I think you'll find that viewing the surface through high magnification, as you will hopefully see in this book, will not only make the distinction of key varieties easier, but will also prove to be part of the fun of the hobby.

Enjoy your journey into the world of coin collecting. It's a great hobby and one full of opportunities that go well beyond the possibility to make money. Most of all enjoy the hunt.

— Robert R. Van Ryzin

HALF CENTS

LIBERTY CAP (1793-1797)

Head facing left (1793)

Designer: Henry Voigt. Size: 22 mm. Weight: 6.74 g. Composition: 100 percent copper.

Alexander Hamilton is largely credited for the introduction of the nation's smallest denomination coin, the half cent. Hamilton proposed the denomination in his 1791 "Report on the Establishment of a Mint," claiming that it would aid the poor by allowing merchants to lower prices. Unfortunately, this never happened, and the coin was largely a nuisance.

This first issue is a one-year type, showing Liberty facing left and a Phrygian, or liberty, cap on a pole. It was struck on a thick planchet, and its edge carried the lettering "Two Hundred for a Dollar."

The design is thought to be patterned largely after the 1782 Libertas Americana medal by Augustin Dupre of France.

Although more than 35,000 of the 1795 Liberty Cap half cents were issued, it is scarce in all grades. Due to the high relief of the obverse design, it's often found with weakly struck reverse details.

Head facing right (1794-1797)

Designers: Robert Scot (1794) and John Smith Gardner (1795-1797). Size: 23.50 mm. Weight: 6.74 g (1794-1795) and 5.44 g (1795-1797). Composition: 100 percent copper. Note: Lettered-edge varieties of this type have "Two Hundred for a Dollar" inscribed around the edge. "Punctuated date" varieties have a comma after the "1" in the date. A 1797 "1 above 1" variety has a second "1" above the first "1" in the date.

Redesigned in 1794 by Mint Engraver Robert Scot, the half cent displayed Liberty facing to the right with a Phrygian cap on a pole. The beaded border gave way to a serrated border. A modification to Scot's design credited to John Smith Gardner showed a smaller head on the coins from 1795 until 1797.

The first pieces of this type bore the edge lettering "Two Hundred for a Dollar," which was subsequently dropped. Due to increasing prices of copper, the weight of the half cent was lowered in 1795 from 6.74 grams for the so-called thick-planchet coinage to 5.44 grams for the thin-planchet strikes.

This type includes a number of famous varieties, such as the 1795 and 1796 "no pole" coins. The former is believed to have been the result of a regrinding of the die, and the latter, simply a mistake. Both are rarities.

The increasing price and inadequate supply of copper also caused the Mint to turn to overstriking privately issued tokens or cut down spoiled cents. The 1795- and 1797-dated half cents are sometimes found struck over tokens issued in 1794 and 1795 by the New York firm of Talbot, Allum & Lee.

DRAPED BUST (1800-1808)

Designer: Robert Scot. Size: 23.50 mm. Weight: 5.44 g. Composition: 100 percent copper. Note: The wreath on the reverse was redesigned slightly in 1802, resulting in "reverse of 1800" and "reverse of 1802" varieties. The 1804 "stems" varieties have stems extending from the wreath above and on both sides of the fraction on the reverse. On the 1804 "crosslet 4" variety, a serif appears at the far right of the crossbar in the "4" in the date. Varieties of the 1805 strikes are distinguished by the size of the "5" in the date. Varieties of the 1806 strikes are distinguished by the size of the "6" in the date.

No half cents were coined dated 1798 or 1799. Beginning with the 1800-dated coinage of half cents, the Draped Bust design by Robert Scot was used, which had been introduced in 1795 on the silver dollar.

Much of the coinage of this type, including the 1800-dated pieces and all of the 1802-dated half cents, was struck on cut down spoiled cent planchets.

Varieties were the rule and not the exception. The 1804, for example, comes in "plain 4," "crosslet 4," "stemless wreath" and "stems in wreath" varieties.

Perhaps the most famous is the 1804 "Spiked Chin" variety, which gained its name from an additional thorn-like spike protruding from Liberty's chin, probably the result of an accidental slip of the engraver's tool.

CLASSIC HEAD (1809-1836)

Designer: John Reich. Size: 23.50 mm. Weight: 5.44 g. Composition: 100 percent copper.

In 1807, John Reich was hired as Assistant Engraver and began a redesign of the nation's coinage. His Classic Head design of Liberty appeared on the cent in 1808 and on the half cent in 1809.

Mintage of the half cent was halted after 1811 and would not resume until 1825.

The 1811 half cent, 63,140 of which were struck, is considered scarce in all grades and a true rarity in uncirculated condition. Even rarer is an unofficial restrike of the 1811 half cent, which used a reverse of 1802, apparently struck in the late 1850s. About one dozen are thought to exist.

Coinage would again be halted after 1829 and would not resume until 1831, with a design modified by Chief Engraver William Kneass and a raised rim created by the introduction of new equipment.

The 1831 date is another rarity, with most known specimens in proof. Restrikes were made in the late 1850s in "large berries" and "small berries" varieties.

The 1836 coinage is known only in proof, with restrikes made in the late 1850s.

BRAIDED HAIR (1840-1857)

Designer: Christian Gobrecht. Size: 23 mm. Weight: 5.44 g. Composition: 100 percent copper.

Coinage of half cents from 1840 through 1848 was in proof only, with no coins released into circulation. Modifications to the design are credited to Christian Gobrecht, who joined the Mint's service in 1836 as an engraver.

All of these dates are rare and all were restruck in the late 1850s. Coinage for circulation did not begin again until 1849 and would continue through 1857.

No coins were struck for circulation in 1852, although a Mint-produced restrike in proof exists.

CENTS

FLOWING HAIR (1793)

Chain Reverse (1793)

Designer: Henry Voigt. Size: 26-27 mm. Weight: 13.48 g. Composition: 100 percent copper.

Significantly larger than cents found in circulation today, the large cent was first coined in 1793 in two major varieties. Both varieties featured a chain with 15 links on the reverse. One displays the word "America" completely; the other gives only "Ameri."

The design, by Henry Voigt, brought the Mint immediate criticism. Some suggested that the chain, which was meant to be emblematic of unity, was a bad omen for liberty. The rather frightened portrayal of Liberty on the obverse was also subject to comment. The edge displayed a vine-and-bars decoration.

Both varieties are generally found only in low grades and struck on poor quality copper.

Wreath Reverse (1793)

Designer: Henry Voigt. Size: 26-27 mm. Weight: 13.48 g. Composition: 100 percent copper.

Criticism of the chain cent reverse appearing on the first U.S. large cent was likely the cause of the introduction of a new design with a remodeled Liberty on the obverse and a wreath on the reverse. All had a raised rim to protect the design and either a vine-and-bars design on the edge or the lettering "One Hundred for a Dollar."

A great rarity of this type is the so-called "strawberry leaf" variety, with a sprig between the date and Liberty unlike those found on other specimens. Only a few are known to exist.

LIBERTY CAP (1793-1796)

Designer: Joseph Wright (1793-1795) and John Smith Gardner (1795-1796). Size: 29 mm. Weight: 13.48 g (1793-1795) and 10.89 g (1795-1796). Composition: 100 percent copper. Note: The heavier pieces were struck on thicker planchets. The Liberty design on the obverse was revised slightly in 1794, but the 1793 design was used on some 1794 strikes. A 1795 "lettered edge" variety has "One Hundred for a Dollar" and a leaf inscribed on the edge.

After changing the design twice in 1793, the Mint did it a third time with the introduction of the Liberty Cap design by Joseph Wright. This new design showed Liberty facing right and a Phrygian cap on a pole. It is believed to be patterned after the Libertas Americana medal struck by France in honor of the American Revolution.

The 1794 date is especially popular among large-cent collectors due to the number of varieties that exist and the extreme difficulty of completing a set. One of the most famous is the 1794 "starred reverse" cent on which the engraver for an unknown reason placed 94 five-pointed stars between the denticles on the coin's reverse.

The 1795-dated cents come in lettered edge and plain edge, the latter having been struck on thinner planchets. The high cost of copper caused Congress to lower the standard weight of the large cent from 208 grains to 168 grains in that year.

Also generally included under this design type is a piece known to collectors as the "Jefferson Head" cent. This rarity was apparently struck outside of the Mint, but with congressional authorization, by John Harper as a coinage proposal during a period in which the Mint was under regular attack for its expenditures.

DRAPED BUST (1796-1807)

Designer: Robert Scot. Size: 29 mm. Weight: 10.89 g. Composition: 100 percent copper. Note: An 1801 "3 errors" variety has the fraction on the reverse reading "1/000," has one stem extending from the wreath above and on both sides of the fraction on the reverse, and has the "United" in "United States of America" looking like "linited."

In 1796, in the wake of the design change implemented on the silver dollar the prior year, Robert Scot's Draped Bust design was introduced on the large cent. The design was modeled after a Gilbert Stuart drawing.

The 1799 cent is a famous rarity, with many of the known examples struck on rough, pitted planchets and in low grade. The 1804 is another rarity of this series, generally found in low grade and struck on porous planchets. Restrikes of this date are also known, and were produced in the late 1850s from original, discarded Mint dies.

CLASSIC HEAD (1808-1814)

Designer: John Reich. Size: 29 mm. Weight: 10.89 g. Composition: 100 percent copper.

After he was assigned to improve the quality of U.S. coin designs, Mint engraver John Reich created a portrait of Liberty that would eventually be used in variations on other copper, silver and gold denominations.

A number of varieties and overdates highlight this design, with many dates struck on dark and porous planchets. No cents were minted in 1815 due to a shortage of copper.

CORONET (1816-1839)

Designer: Robert Scot. Size: 28-29 mm. Weight: 10.89 g. Composition: 100 percent copper.
Note: The 1817 strikes have either 13 or 15 stars on the obverse.

Robert Scot again redesigned the cent in 1816. A new, slimmer Liberty wearing a coronet with the word "Liberty" inscribed on it would appear on the cent's obverse through 1839. The dates 1816 through 1820 are considered plentiful in uncirculated condition due to the Randall Hoard, a keg of large cents discovered in Georgia following the Civil War and eventually sold to John Randall.

A number of minor varieties and overdates spice this type.

BRAIDED HAIR (1839-1857)

Designer: Christian Gobrecht. Size: 27.50 mm. Weight: 10.89 g. Composition: 100 percent copper. Note: 1840 and 1842 strikes are known with both small and large dates. 1855 and 1856 strikes are known with both slanting and upright "5s" in the date. A slightly larger Liberty head and large reverse lettering were used beginning in 1843. One 1844 variety used the old obverse with the new reverse.

Redesign of the cent began in 1835 after the death of former Chief Engraver Robert Scot. A number of transitional designs and colorful varieties were the result. Examples include the 1839 strikes that came to be known to large-cent collectors under the sobriquets Silly Head, Booby Head and Petite Head.

Christian Gobrecht, a bank-note engraver before entering the Mint's employ, is generally credited with the Braided Hair design that came into use in 1839. It was used for the remainder of the large-cent series.

Besides design varieties, the Braided Hair type includes a number of engraving blunders, generally credited to James B. Longacre, who succeeded Gobrecht in 1844 as Chief Engraver. The most dramatic are the 1844/81 and 1851/81 overdates.

FLYING EAGLE (1856-1858)

Designer: James B. Longacre. Size: 19 mm. Weight: 4.67 g.
Composition: 88 percent copper, 12 percent nickel.

Unpopular and costly to produce, the 27.5-millimeter large cent was abandoned in 1857 in favor of a small cent. The new small cent, comprised of 88 percent copper and 12 percent nickel, measured only 19 millimeters. It was eagerly welcomed by the public.

Coinage for 1856 was in the form of a pattern issue. It has since largely come to be accepted as part of the regular U.S. coinage series. This was likely due to the distribution of more than 600 1856 Flying Eagle cents to congressmen and others. Restrikes were made in 1858 and 1859.

Coinage began in earnest in 1857, with the Mint accepting large cents and foreign silver in exchange for the new cent.

Mintage of the regular-issue Flying Eagle cent was high, with 17.45 million struck in 1857 and an additional 24.6 million minted in 1858. The 1858 issue includes large- and small-letter varieties.

Although the new small cent was popular with the public, the design and the metallic composition led to striking problems, and the Flying Eagle design was dropped after only two years of regular-issue coinage.

INDIAN HEAD (1859-1909)

Copper-Nickel Composition, Laurel Wreath (1859)

Designer: James B. Longacre. Size: 19 mm. Weight: 4.67 g.
Composition: 88 percent copper, 12 percent nickel.

First issues of the Indian Head cent, designed by James B. Longacre, displayed Liberty wearing an Indian headdress on the obverse. A laurel wreath is shown on the reverse. This wreath would be abandoned the following year in favor of an oak wreath. Mintage of this one-year type was 36.4 million.

Copper-Nickel Composition, Oak Wreath (1860-1864)

Designer: James B. Longacre. Size: 19 mm. Weight: 4.67 g.
Composition: 88 percent copper, 12 percent nickel.

An oak wreath and shield design graced the reverse of the Indian Head cent for most of its coinage. Mintages were high, with the peak year in 1863 when 49.84 million were struck. The low years were 1861, with 10.1 million struck, and 1864, with 13.74 million struck.

Bronze Composition (1864-1909)

Designer: James B. Longacre. Size: 19 mm. Weight: 3.11 g.
Composition: 95 percent copper, 5 percent tin and zinc.

The Mint turned to a bronze composition for the cent in 1864 as a result of public hoarding during the Civil War. Bronze was more readily available, and the metal was easier to work with than nickel. The new cents were comprised of 95 percent copper and 5 percent tin and zinc, and were thinner and lighter than the copper-nickel cents.

The first-year issue came with or without an "L" representing the designer, James B. Longacre. It is located between the hair and lower feather of the Indian's headdress. The "with L" specimens command a premium. The 1873 date is known in both "closed 3" and "open 3" varieties.

A change in the design hub in 1886 created another two varieties. The first shows the final feather of the headdress pointing between the "IC" in "America." Those struck through the remainder of that year and the rest of the Indian Head series have the feather pointing between the "CA" of "America."

The series' best-known rarity is the 1877, with a mintage of 852,500. It is often found weakly struck.

Branch-mint coinage of cents began in 1908 at the San Francisco Mint with the low-mintage 1908-S. The 1909-S is the lowest mintage regular-issue Indian Head cent (309,000 struck) and a premium coin in all grades.

LINCOLN (1909 TO DATE)

Wheat Reverse,
Bronze Composition (1909-1942)

Designer: Victor D. Brenner. Size: 19 mm. Weight: 3.11 g.
Composition: 95 percent copper, 5 percent tin and zinc.

The Lincoln cent holds the distinction of being the first regular-issue U.S. coin to bear the portrait of a U.S. president. Designed by Victor D. Brenner, it was released to commemorate the 100th anniversary of Abraham Lincoln's birth. The reverse design featured wheat stalks. With some minor modifications, this design was used through 1958.

When released in 1909, the Lincoln cent bore Brenner's initials, "V.D.B.," at the bottom of the coin's reverse. Criticism of the prominent placement of the engraver's initials led to their deletion in the same year. This created one of the hobby's most popular varieties, the 1909-S "V.D.B.," with a mintage of 484,000. Brenner's initials would not be restored again until 1918, and then only on the truncation of Lincoln's shoulder.

Other keys of this design type include the 1914-D, 1922 "no D" and the 1931-S. The 1922 "no D" is so termed because of a filled die, which caused some Denver Mint coins to appear without the "D" mintmark. As no cents were struck at the Philadelphia Mint in that year, the 1922 "no D" became a popular variety.

Many other dates are found weakly struck and elusive in high grade with full mint red.

Steel Composition (1943)

Designer: Victor D. Brenner. Size: 19 mm. Weight: 2.70 g. Composition: Steel coated with zinc.

In 1943, wartime demand for copper led to the introduction of a zinc-coated steel cent, which would be used until the following year. Many today are found corroded. Others have been reprocessed: the top layer of zinc stripped from the surface, re-plated, and then sold to collectors.

Mintages on the 1943 zinc-coated steel cents were very high and examples are common. The 1943-S, with a mintage of 191.6 million, carries the highest premium of the three mints that struck the coin, though it is slight.

A very small number of 1943-dated cents struck on copper planchets were inadvertently minted and are great rarities. Unfortunately, a number of steel cents have been plated with copper by those hoping to pass the coins off as copper cents. These can be detected by attraction to a magnet. On others, authentication is mandatory.

Copper-Zinc Composition (1944-1958)

Designer: Victor D. Brenner. Size: 19 mm. Weight: 3.11 g. Composition: 95 percent copper, 5 percent zinc 1944-1946; 95 percent copper, 5 percent tin and zinc 1947-1958.

Copper returned to the cent in 1944, in the form of metal salvaged from spent World War II shell casings. Shell casings were used as a copper source through 1946.

The most famous variety of this type is the 1955 doubled die, which was the result of the use of an accidentally doubled obverse die.

Memorial Reverse,
Bronze Composition (1959-1962)

Designer: Victor D. Brenner, obverse; Frank Gasparro, reverse.
Size: 19 mm. Weight: 3.11 g. Composition: 95 percent copper, 5 percent tin and zinc.

In 1959, the wheat-ear reverse was abandoned on the cent in favor of a depiction of the Lincoln Memorial, a design meant to commemorate the 150th anniversary of Abraham Lincoln's birth.

This type includes two popular but low premium varieties that are still occasionally found in circulation: the 1960 small- and large-date cents. They were struck at both the Denver and Philadelphia mints.

Memorial Reverse,
Brass Composition (1962-1982)

Designer: Victor D. Brenner, obverse; Frank Gasparro, reverse. Size: 19 mm.
Weight: 3.11 g. Composition: 95 percent copper, 5 percent zinc. Note: The date was
modified in 1970 and 1982, resulting in large- and small-date varieties. A 1972
doubled-die cent shows doubling of "In God We Trust."

In 1969, a limited number of cents were released from the San Francisco Mint with a doubled obverse. In 1972, the Philadelphia Mint also released a cent with a doubled obverse. Both exhibit wide doubling of the features.

Though of much lesser value, small- and large-date varieties of the 1970-S are also well known to collectors. The small-date variety was a premium coin. It can also be found on proof strikes.

In 1974, more than 1.5 million Lincoln cents were minted in aluminum as an experiment with the cheaper metal. Almost all were destroyed. A few pieces, given out to members of Congress, were not returned and apparently remain in private hands.

Copper-Plated Zinc
Composition (1982 to 2008)

Designer: Victor D. Brenner, obverse; Frank Gasparro, reverse. Size: 19 mm. Weight: 2.50 g. Composition: 99.20 percent zinc, .80 percent copper. Note: A 1983 doubled-die reverse shows doubling on "United States of America" and "One Cent." A 1984 doubled-die cent shows doubling on Lincoln's ear. A 1992 variety has a "close AM" in "America" on the coin's reverse in which the letters almost touch. The Philadelphia version is apparently the rarest of the known 1992-P and –D "close AM" business strikes.

In 1982, the rising cost of copper led the Mint to turn to a copper-plated zinc composition, although problems with discoloring hark back to the 1943 zinc-coated steel cents.

Lincoln Bicentennial,
Log Cabin Reverse (2009)

Designer: Victor D. Brenner, obverse; Richard Masters, James Licaretz, reverse. Size: 19 mm. Weight: 2.50 g. Composition: 99.20 percent zinc, .80 percent copper.

The first in a four-coin release honoring the bicentennial of Abraham Lincoln's birth featured a log cabin. The cabin represented Lincoln's birth on Feb. 12, 1809 in rural Kentucky.

Lincoln Bicentennial,
Lincoln Seated on Log Reverse (2009)

Designer: Victor D. Brenner, obverse; Charles Vickers, reverse. Size: 19 mm. Weight: 2.50 g. Composition: 99.20 percent zinc, .80 percent copper.

Abraham Lincoln is shown seated on a log, reading a book during a break from rail splitting during his youth in Indiana.

Lincoln Bicentennial, Lincoln Standing
Before Illinois State House Reverse (2009)

Designer: Victor D. Brenner, obverse; Joel Iskowitz and Don Everhart, reverse. Size: 19 mm. Weight: 2.50 g. Composition: 99.20 percent zinc, .80 percent copper.

Abraham Lincoln's professional life in Illinois is reflected on this coin showing the future president before the Illinois state house. Lincoln was elected to the Illinois General Assembly in 1834.

Lincoln Bicentennial,
Capitol Building Reverse (2009)

Designer: Victor D. Brenner, obverse; Susan Gamble and Joseph Menna, reverse. Size: 19 mm. Weight: 2.50 g. Composition: 99.20 percent zinc, .80 percent copper.

The U.S. Capitol Building is depicted on the fourth cent released in the Lincoln Bicentennial series. The Capitol is lacking its dome, as it was still under construction during Lincoln's first term in office as the 16th president of the United States.

Shield Reverse
(2010 to date)

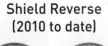

Designer: Victor D. Brenner, obverse; Lyndall Bass and Joseph Menna, reverse. Size: 19 mm. Weight: 2.50 g. Composition: 99.20 percent zinc, .80 percent copper.

A shield design was placed on the reverse of the cent beginning in 2010. It represents Abraham Lincoln's efforts to keep the Union together and carries the motto "E Pluribus Unum" and the denomination on a banner. The union shield dates back to the 18th century. The 13 stripes on the shield represent the original 13 states to join the Union.

2
CENTS

2-CENT PIECE (1864-1873)

Designer: James B. Longacre. Size: 23 mm. Weight: 6.22 g.
Composition: 95 percent copper, 5 percent tin and zinc.

The suspension of specie payments in the early 1860s and the outbreak of the Civil War led to the hoarding of all precious metals, including the copper-nickel cent. Mint Director James Pollock believed that the introduction of a 2-cent bronze piece would be convenient to the public and help alleviate the coin shortage.

Unfortunately, the public found little use for the new denomination. After opening mintages in the range of 20 million per year, production of the 2-cent piece dropped to a scant 65,000 in 1872, the last year of coinage for circulation.

A small number of proofs were made the following year for the benefit of collectors before the denomination was officially dropped by the Coinage Act of 1873.

The 2-cent piece holds the distinction of being the first regular-issue U.S. coin to bear the motto "In God We Trust," which would eventually come into standard use.

The 1864 strike is found in small- and large-motto varieties.

3
CENTS

SILVER 3-CENT PIECE (1851-1873)

Type 1 (1851-1853)

Designer: James B. Longacre. Size: 14 mm. Weight: .8 g.
Composition: 75 percent silver (.0193 oz.), 25 percent copper.

The smallest U.S. silver coin by diameter, the silver 3-cent piece, was authorized in 1851 by an act of Congress. Measuring only 14 millimeters, it was meant to serve as a convenient method to purchase the newly issued 3-cent postage stamps.

The first design type, struck from 1851 to 1853, has a six-pointed star on the obverse with no lines bordering it. Unlike other silver coins, which were issued in a standard of 90 percent silver and 10 percent copper, the Type 1 silver 3-cent pieces were minted in 75 percent silver and 25 percent copper.

This type included the only branch-mint coinage of the silver 3-cent piece, with 720,000 struck in 1851 at the New Orleans Mint. It is also the scarcest date.

Type II (1854-1858)

Designer: James B. Longacre. Size: 14 mm. Weight: .75 g.
Composition: 90 percent silver (.0217 oz.), 10 percent copper.

In 1854, the design of the silver 3-cent piece was changed from a borderless star to one showing three lines around the star on the obverse. An olive sprig and arrows were added to the reverse.

These and subsequent silver 3-cent pieces, would conform with higher denomination silver coins by reducing the copper alloy from 25 percent to 10 percent. The weight was lowered from .80 gram to .75 gram.

Type II silver 3-cent pieces are generally found weakly struck.

Type III (1859-1873)

Designer: James B. Longacre. Size: 14 mm. Weight: .75 g.
Composition: 90 percent silver (..0217 oz.), 10 percent copper.

In 1859, the design of the silver 3-cent was changed for the third time, probably due to striking problems with the first two designs. The Type III design featured just two lines around the star instead of the three lines found on the Type II coins.

At first, mintages of the silver 3-cent pieces were high, with the peak at 18,663,500 in 1852. But by the 1860s, in the wake of the suspension of specie payments and the Civil War, mintages began to fall off, as all precious metals were hoarded.

After 1862, coinage of the silver 3-cent piece plummeted to a low in 1872, when only 1,950 were struck. During the final year of coinage, only proofs were minted.

NICKEL 3-CENT PIECE (1865-1889)

Designer: James B. Longacre. Size: 17.9 mm. Weight: 1.94 g.
Composition: 75 percent copper, 25 percent nickel.

Composed of 75 percent copper and 25 percent nickel, but with a silvery appearance, the nickel 3-cent piece was released in 1865. They were minted largely to replace the unpopular 3-cent fractional paper notes, many of which had become ragged and torn since their authorization in 1863. The nickel 3-cent coins were paid out in exchange for redemption of the paper notes.

The first-year mintage was a high 11.382 million, but afterward, mintages began to drop. The dates from 1884 through 1887 were especially low and carry strong premiums in all grades. Only proofs were struck in 1877, 1878 and in 1886.

The high percentage of nickel used in the composition caused striking problems, leading many dates in the series to be found weakly struck.

HALF
DIMES

FLOWING HAIR (1794-1795)

Designer: Robert Scot. Size: 16.5 mm. Weight: 1.35 g.
Composition: 89.24 percent silver (.0388 oz.), 10.72 percent copper.

Mint Engraver Robert Scot's depiction of Liberty facing right appeared on the first half dimes struck at the U.S. Mint. The half dime's reverse featured a small eagle within a wreath. Combined mintage of both dates came to only 86,416, all of which were actually struck in 1795. Both dates are scarce and rare in uncirculated condition. Many varieties exist.

DRAPED BUST (1794-1805)

Small-eagle reverse (1796-1797)

Designer: Robert Scot. Size: 16.5 mm. Weight: 1.35 g.
Composition: 89.24 percent silver (.0388 oz.), 10.72 percent copper.

Robert Scot's Draped Bust Liberty, modeled after an original drawing by Gilbert Stuart, began appearing on the half dime in 1796.

The most famous of several 1796 varieties is one in which the word "Liberty" appears as "Likerty"– due to worn dies.

Heraldic eagle reverse (1800-1805)

Designer: Robert Scot. Size: 16.5 mm. Weight: 1.35 g.
Composition: 89.24 percent silver (.0388 oz.), 10.72 percent copper.

No half dimes were struck from 1798 through 1799. By the time coinage resumed in 1800, the small-eagle reverse had been replaced by a heraldic eagle.

Like the 1796 coinage, a variety of 1800 strikes display the word "Liberty" as "Likerty." This time, however, a defective letter punch, not wear to the die, is thought to have been the problem.

The 1802 half dime is a famous U.S. rarity, with a believed mintage of 3,060. Of the small number of specimens still in existence, most are in low grade and often weakly struck.

No half dimes were struck in 1804. Coinage resumed in 1805, with 15,600 half dimes minted.

CAPPED BUST (1829-1837)

Designer: William Kneass. Size: 15.5 mm. Weight: 1.35 g.
Composition: 89.24 percent silver (.0388 oz.), 10.72 percent copper. Note: Design modifications
in 1835, 1836 and 1837 resulted in variety combinations with large and small dates, and large
and small "5C." inscriptions on the reverse.

Half dime coinage was stopped after 1805 and would not resume until 1829. The new coinage used John Reich's Capped Bust design, which was already appearing on the other silver denominations.

This would be the first half dime to express the denomination, shown as "5C." below the eagle on the reverse.

SEATED LIBERTY (1837-1873)

No stars around rim (1837-1838)

Designer: Christian Gobrecht. Size: 15.5 mm. Weight: 1.34 g.
Composition: 90 percent silver (.0388 oz.), 10 percent copper.

In a move aimed at unifying coinage designs, Christian Gobrecht's Seated Liberty design was placed on the half dime in 1837. The design first made its appearance in 1836 on the dollar.

The 1837 half dime is found in both small- and large-date varieties.

Stars around rim (1838-1853)

Designer: Christian Gobrecht. Size: 15.5 mm. Weight: 1.34 g. Composition: 90 percent silver (.0388 oz.), 10 percent copper. Note: Two varieties of the 1838 are distinguished by the size of the stars on the obverse. An 1839-O with reverse of 1838-O variety was struck from rusted reverse dies. The result is a bumpy surface on this variety's reverse.

In 1838, 13 stars were added to the obverse design of the half dime. Pieces from 1837 through 1840 lack drapery from Liberty's left elbow. The drapery was added in 1840 as the result of design remodeling by Robert Ball Hughes.

The 1840 half dime is known in "no drapery" and "drapery" versions, struck by both the Philadelphia and the New Orleans mints. The drapery varieties of that date had lower mintages and bring higher premiums.

Other varieties include the 1848 medium- and large-date coins and the 1849 with overdates of 9/6 and 9/8.

The 1846, of which 27,000 were coined, is a premium key in all grades. Also very scarce is the 1853-O without arrows at the date.

Arrows at date (1853-1855)

Designer: Christian Gobrecht. Size: 15.5 mm. Weight: 1.24 g. Composition: 90 percent silver (.0362 oz.), 10 percent copper.

The discovery of gold in California in 1848 drove the price of silver up, and as their bullion value exceeded face value, silver coins began to disappear from circulation. Those coins that weren't melted or shipped overseas were simply hoarded.

Attempting to rectify the problem, the Mint Act of 1853 reduced the weight of all silver coins, with the exception of the silver dollar, to fall in line with a subsidiary dollar of 384 grains.

First-year mintage at Philadelphia of the reduced-weight half dime was 13.210 million. The low-mintage date is the 1855-O, of which 600,000 were struck.

Arrows at date removed (1856-1859)

Designer: Christian Gobrecht. Size: 15.5 mm. Weight: 1.24 g.
Composition: 90 percent silver (.0362 oz.), 10 percent copper.

In 1856, the arrows were dropped from the date area, although the weight of the half dime remained at the new lower level adopted in 1853.

A famous variety is the 1858 over inverted date, a Mint blunder generally credited to the hand of U.S. Mint Chief Engraver James B. Longacre, who made a number of such mistakes during his tenure.

Obverse legend (1860-1873)

Designer: Christian Gobrecht. Size: 15.5 mm. Weight: 1.24 g.
Composition: 90 percent silver (.0362 oz.), 10 percent copper.

In 1860, the legend "United States of America" replaced stars on the obverse of the half dime. A new wreath design was employed for the reverse.

Philadelphia strikes from 1863-1867 are all low mintage and scarce in all grades.

The 1870-S half dime is a classic rarity. No specimens were known to exist until 1978 when one was discovered in a dealer's junk box and brought to the attention of the collecting public in an article in the Sept. 9, 1978 issue of *Numismatic News*.

Although coinage of the silver half dime continued through 1873, the coin had become unpopular. The introduction and public acceptance of the Shield 5-cent piece, comprised of 75 percent copper and 25 percent nickel, along with the problems of keeping silver in circulation led to the elimination of the half dime by the Coinage Act of 1873.

5
CENTS

SHIELD (1866-1883)

Variety 1 (1866-1867)

Designer: James B. Longacre. Size: 20.50 mm. Weight: 5 g.
Composition: 75 percent copper, 25 percent nickel.

Much like the nickel 3-cent piece, the nation's first base-metal 5-cent piece was suggested as a substitute for 5-cent fractional notes by Mint Director James Pollock.

The federally issued Fractional Currency notes were one of a number of wartime substitutes for scarce precious-metal coinage. After the war, the notes continued to circulate, even though the worn and tattered paper money were unpopular with the public.

The nickel 5-cent pieces show rays between the stars on those struck in 1866 and a portion of those minted in 1867.

Striking problems with the "with rays" design evidently led to its replacement in 1867, but not before some 2 million of the 1867 "with rays" coins were struck. Mintage of the "no rays" variety far exceeded that of its predecessor, reaching 28.9 million. The "with rays" variety is a scarce and popular coin.

Variety 2 (1867-1883)

Designer: James B. Longacre. Size: 20.50 mm. Weight: 5 g.
Composition: 75 percent copper, 25 percent nickel.

The Variety 2 coin sported no rays between the stars on the coin's reverse. Unlike the 3-cent piece, the nickel, as the 5-cent piece came to be known, was readily accepted. It continues to be a useful part of the nation's coinage system today. Notable dates of this type include the 1871, with a mintage of 561,000; the 1873 "closed 3" variety; and the 1879-1881 dates, all of which sported low mintages. No 5-cent pieces were struck for circulation in 1877 and 1878.

LIBERTY HEAD (1883-1913)

Variety 1 (1883)

Designer: Charles E. Barber. Size: 21.20 mm. Weight: 5 g.
Composition: 75 percent copper, 25 percent nickel.

Designed by Mint Engraver Charles Barber, the first Liberty Head nickels bore only a Roman numeral "V" within a wreath and failed to include the word "Cents." The design flaw was soon noted by the unscrupulous, who found the 5-cent piece's similarity in size to the gold $5 useful. It soon became prey to gold-plating so it could be passed at the higher value.

Some 5.48 million of the 1883-dated "centless" coins were struck before the design was changed to feature the word "cents" below the wreath.

Variety 2 (1883-1913)

Designer: Charles E. Barber. Size: 21.20 mm. Weight: 5 g.
Composition: 75 percent copper, 25 percent nickel.

In 1883, having realized the problem caused by not including the word "cents" below the Roman numeral "V" on the Liberty Head nickel's reverse, the Mint altered the design to include the denomination.

Among the high premium dates of the 1883-1913 Variety 2 coins are the 1885, 1886 and 1912-S.

The most famous coin in the series is the 1913 Liberty Head nickel. It was apparently clandestinely struck by a Mint employee after the order to change to the Buffalo nickel design had been received. Only five 1913 Liberty Head nickels are thought to exist, all of which are proofs.

BUFFALO (1913-1938)

Variety 1 (1913)

Designer: James Earle Fraser. Size: 21.20 mm. Weight: 5 g.
Composition: 75 percent copper, 25 percent nickel.

Popularly termed the Buffalo nickel after the reverse image (which is actually a bison and not a buffalo), the Buffalo nickel was a product of an era of coinage redesign inspired by President Theodore Roosevelt.

The obverse bore a composition portrait of a Plains Indian prepared by James Earle Fraser from various models. Although it not know for certain who the models were, the most likely candidates were Iron Tail, a Sioux; Two Moons, a Cheyenne; and Adoeette (Big Tree), a Kiowa.

First examples of the Buffalo nickel showed the bison on a raised mound. The design was found to wear quickly and was replaced that same year to place the denomination in recess to protect it from wear.

Variety 2 (1913-1938)

Designer: James Earle Fraser. Size: 21.20 mm. Weight: 5 g.
Composition: 75 percent copper, 25 percent nickel.

Because first examples of the Buffalo nickel were subject to wear in the denomination area, the design was changed from the Variety 1 mound design of 1913 to the Variety 2. Spanning from 1913 until 1938, Variety 2 featured the denomination in recess.

Even this change could not escape the fact that the entire design, although aesthetically pleasing, was in too high relief for high-speed coinage. Therefore, many dates are found weakly struck. This is particularly noticeable on the coinage of Denver and San Francisco. The 1926-D is a notorious example.

This type includes one of the 20th century's most famous overdates, the 1918/7-D, and a 1916 with doubled obverse. Also sought after is the 1937-D "three-legged" Buffalo nickel, which, due to excessive grinding of a damaged die, lacks part of the right front foreleg of the bison design.

An interesting overmintmark, the 1938-D/S, apparently occurred when planned coinage at the San Francisco Mint did not happen and a previously prepared die was pressed into service.

JEFFERSON (1938 TO DATE)

Prewar composition (1938-1942)

Designer: Felix Schlag. Size: 21.20 mm. Weight: 5 g.
Composition: 75 percent copper, 25 percent nickel.

Thomas Jefferson, whose efforts to establish a decimal coinage system are still enjoyed today, was placed on the 5-cent piece beginning in 1938. Jefferson's home, Monticello, is depicted on the reverse.

One interesting issue of 1939 shows doubling on the legend "Monticello" and "Five Cents." Another, struck in 1942, shows the "D" mintmark over a horizontal "D."

The 1939-D, with a mintage of 3.514 million, is generally considered the key date.

Wartime composition (1942-1945)

Designer: Felix Schlag. Size: 21.20 mm. Weight: 5 g.
Composition: 56 percent copper, 35 percent silver (.0563 oz.), 9 percent manganese.

In 1942, need for more supplies of the metal nickel to aid in the war effort led to the issuance of a 5-cent piece containing 35 percent silver.

In order to be able to readily identify the new 5-cent pieces from those containing 25 percent nickel, the mintmark was placed prominently above the dome of Monticello. For the first time a "P" was used to distinguish those coins struck at Philadelphia.

A significant overdate, the 1943/2-P, is known in the wartime composition.

Prewar composition resumed (1946-2003)

Designer: Felix Schlag. Size: 21.20 mm. Weight: 5 g.
Composition: 75 percent copper, 25 percent nickel.

In 1946, the 5-cent piece's pre-war 75 percent copper, 25 percent nickel composition was restored. The mintmark was again placed to the side of Monticello.

The postwar series features a number of overmintmark coins, including the 1949-D/S, 1954-S/D and the 1955-D/S.

In 1965, the Mint, facing a coinage shortage, opted to leave mintmarks off U.S. coins. It unjustly feared that coin collectors were aiding in the disappearance of coins from circulation.

Mintmarks would again be placed on U.S. coins beginning in 1968. On the 5-cent piece, the mintmark returned in a larger form to a new location on the obverse. In 1966, designer Felix Schlag's initials were added below the bust of Jefferson.

Specialists in the series often collect these nickels for the number and fullness of the porch steps on Monticello, which are generally weakly defined.

Modifications, noticeable in strengthening design details of Monticello, also led to the creation of collectible varieties in 1967, 1971 and 1977.

Westward Journey, Jefferson era Peace Medal design (2004)

Designer: Felix Schlag obverse; Norman E. Nemeth reverse. Size: 21.20 mm. Weight: 5 g. Composition: 75 percent copper, 25 percent nickel.

The first in the Westward Journey series of nickels showed the design of an Indian Peace Medal commissioned for the Lewis and Clark Expedition. It depicts two hands clasped in friendship.

One of the cuffs of the hands is a military uniform (for the United States) and the other cuff has a silver band with beads and a stylized eagle (for the American Indians).

Westward Journey, Lewis and Clark keelboat (2004)

Designer: Felix Schlag, obverse; Al Maletsky, reverse. Size: 21.20 mm. Weight: 5 g. Composition: 75 percent copper, 25 percent nickel.

A keelboat in full sail, with Lewis and Clark at the bow, appears on this 2005 Westward Journey 5-cent piece.

Westward Journey,
Jefferson large profile right;
American Bison right (2005)

Designer: Joe Fitzgerald, Don Everhart II, obverse; Jamie Franki, Norman E. Nemeth, reverse.
Size: 21.20 mm. Weight: 5 g. Composition: 75 percent copper, 25 percent nickel.

The obverse of the Jefferson nickel was redesigned for the 2005 Westward Journey nickel, replacing the Felix Schlag design that had been used since 1938. Still employing the Houdon marble bust of Thomas Jefferson as the inspiration, the new observe shows a side view of the president, with the word "Liberty" based on Jefferson's handwriting. The coin's reverse shows an American bison, in honor of the bison encountered on the Lewis and Clark Expedition as well as their importance to American Indian cultures.

Westward Journey,
Jefferson large profile right;
'Ocean in view! O! The Joy!'
(2005)

Designer: Joe Fitzgerald, Don Everhart II, obverse; Joe Fitzgerald, Donna Weaver, reverse.
Size: 21.20 mm. Weight: 5 g. Composition: 75 percent copper, 25 percent nickel.

"Ocean in view! O! The joy!" appeared on the 2005 Westward Journey nickel marking the journal entry made by Capt. William Clark on Nov. 7, 1805, upon believing the expedition had reached the Pacific Coast. The design, showing the Pacific Ocean, was based on a photograph by Andrew E. Cier.

Jefferson head facing, Monticello, enhanced design (2006 to Date)

Designer: Jamie Franki, Donna Weaver, obverse. Size: 21.20 mm. Weight: 5 g. Composition: 75 percent copper, 25 percent nickel.

In 2006, another new portrait of Thomas Jefferson appeared on the obverse of the 5-cent piece. This one was based on a portrait of Jefferson completed in 1800 by Rembrant Peale. It shows Jefferson at age 57, serving as Vice President just before becoming President. The word "Liberty" appears, based on Jefferson's handwriting. An enhanced design of Monticello returned to the nickel's reverse.

10
CENTS

DRAPED BUST (1797-1807)

Small-eagle reverse (1796-1797)

Designer: Robert Scot. Size: 19 mm. Weight: 2.70 g. Composition: 89.24 percent silver (.0775 oz.), 10.76 percent copper. Note: 1797 strikes have either 13 or 16 stars on the obverse.

Coinage of dimes did not begin until 1796. Versions of Robert Scot's Draped Bust modeled after a Gilbert Stuart drawing had already appeared on the silver dollar and were being adopted for the cent, half dime and quarter dollar. The dime's reverse depicted a small eagle, perched on a cloud, enclosed by a wreath.

Mintages were low for both years of the small-eagle reverse, with 22,135 believed to have been struck bearing the 1796 date and an additional mintage of 25,261 in 1797. Both dates are scarce, high-premium coins.

Heraldic-eagle reverse (1798-1807)

Designer: Robert Scot. Size: 19 mm. Weight: 2.70 g. Composition: 89.24 percent silver (.0775 oz.), 10.76 percent copper. Note: Varieties of the regular 1798 strikes are distinguished by the size of the "8" in the date. The 1805 strikes have either four or five berries on the olive branch held by the eagle.

Robert Scot's heraldic-eagle reverse was teamed with the Draped Bust obverse on the dime beginning in 1798.

Conservation of coinage dies at the first Mint often led to the creation of overdates. A die prepared in a prior year would be re-punched and put into service. The 1798 strikes, for example, can be found with 98/97 and with 16- or 13-star obverses.

The 1804 is found with 13 or 14 stars on the reverse. The latter was created when an 1804 quarter eagle reverse was used on the dime coinage. Most dates of this type were weakly struck. No dimes were coined in 1799 or 1806.

CAPPED BUST (1809-1837)

Large size (1809-1828)

Designer: John Reich. Size: 18.80 mm. Weight: 2.70 g. Composition: 89.24 percent silver (.0775 oz.), 10.76 percent copper. Note: Varieties of the 1814, 1821 and 1828 strikes are distinguished by the size of the numerals in the dates. Varieties of the 1820 are distinguished by the size of the "0" in the date. Overdates of 1823 have either large "Es" or small "Es" in "United States of America" on the reverse.

John Reich's Capped Bust design, which in 1807 had been placed on the half dollar, was introduced on the dime in 1809. It replaced the Draped Bust design, used from 1797 through 1807. No dimes were minted in 1808.

One of several varieties of the Capped Bust coinage occurred when the same reverse die was used in 1814 and again in 1820. The die had "StatesofAmerica" appear without spacing, as one word.

Coinage of the dime was sporadic. No dimes were struck in 1810, 1812, 1813, 1815 through 1819, or in 1826.

The 1822, with a mintage of 100,000, is a key date and scarce in all grades.

Reduced size (1828-1837)

Designer: John Reich. Size: 18.50 mm. Weight: 2.70 g. Composition: 89.24 percent silver (.0775 oz.), 10.76 percent copper. Note: Three varieties of the 1829 strikes and two varieties of the 1830 strikes are distinguished by the size of "10C." on the reverse. An 1833 "high 3" variety has the last "3" in the date higher than the first "3." Two varieties of the 1834 strikes are distinguished by the size of the "4" in the date.

The introduction of new equipment at the Mint and, in particular, the use of a close coinage collar slightly reduced the diameter of the dime and made coinage more unified. The new dime also displayed a raised, beaded border.

Coinage of the dime, which prior to 1828 had been sporadic, became regular. No breaks in the date occur between 1828 and 1837.

SEATED LIBERTY (1837-1891)

No stars (1837-1838)

Designer: Christian Gobrecht. Size: 17.90 mm. Weight: 2.67 g. Composition: 90 percent silver (.0773 oz.), 10 percent copper. Note: Two 1837 varieties are distinguished by the size of the numerals in the date.

Christian Gobrecht's Seated Liberty design was placed on the dime in 1837 without the stars bordering the design that would characterize the issues from 1838-1860.

The rarest coin of this type is the 1838-O, the first branch-mint coinage of dimes. With 406,034 struck, the 1838-O is especially rare in uncirculated grades.

No dimes of this type were struck at Philadelphia in 1838, which had by then turned to coinage of the modified design with stars bordering Liberty.

Stars around rim (1838-1853)

Designer: Christian Gobrecht. Size: 17.90 mm. Weight: 2.67 g. Composition: 90 percent silver (.0773 oz.), 10 percent copper. Note: Two 1838 varieties are distinguished by the size of the stars on the obverse. An 1838 "partial drapery" variety has drapery on Liberty's left elbow. An 1839-O with reverse of 1838-O variety was struck from rusted dies. This variety has a bumpy surface on the reverse.

Beginning in 1838, 13 stars were added to the obverse design of the Seated Liberty dimes struck at the Philadelphia Mint. Coinage of this type would not begin until the following year at the New Orleans facility.

The 1844, known to collectors as the "Orphan Annie" dime, is scarce. Also scarce is the 1846, which is the lowest mintage date of this type. Only 31,300 were struck.

The Philadelphia Mint also struck 95,000 1853 "no arrows" coins at the old standard of 2.67 grams before the reduction of weight of the dime in that year to 2.49 grams.

Arrows at date (1853-1855)

Designer: Christian Gobrecht. Size: 17.90 mm. Weight: 2.49 g. Composition: 90 percent silver (.072), 10 percent copper.

In 1853, the weight of the dime was reduced in an attempt to keep it in circulation. Large supplies of gold from the California gold fields had helped to drive the price of silver up to a point where silver coins were worth more as bullion than their face value. Arrows were added at the date to dimes struck from 1853 through 1855 to denote the weight change.

First-year mintage of the "with arrows" dime was high, at 12.08 million in Philadelphia. By contrast, only 1.1 million were struck in New Orleans.

Mintage at the Philadelphia Mint would drop to 4.47 million the following year, with the New Orleans coinage standing at 1.77 million. The final year of the "with arrows" dime saw 2.075 million coins struck at the Philadelphia Mint.

All are relatively plentiful in lower grades.

Arrows at date removed (1856-1860)

Designer: Christian Gobrecht. Size: 17.90 mm. Weight: 2.49 g. Composition: 90 percent silver (.072), 10 percent copper. Note: Two 1856 varieties are distinguished by the size of the numerals in the date.

In 1856, the arrows were removed from the date area of the dime, even though the weight remained at the new, lower level. In that same year, the San Francisco Mint struck its first dime, with a low mintage of 70,000. This date and the 1859-S are scarce in all grades.

Obverse legend (1860-1873)

Designer: Christian Gobrecht. Size: 17.90 mm. Weight: 2.49 g. Composition: 90 percent silver (.072), 10 percent copper. Note: 1873 "closed-3" and "open-3" varieties are known and are distinguished by the amount of space between the upper left and lower left serifs of the "3" in the date.

In 1860, Mint Chief Engraver James B. Longacre reworked the design of the dime on orders from Mint Director A. Louden Snowden. The inscription "United States of America" was moved to the obverse and a new so-called cereal wreath was placed on the reverse.

A number of rarities exist of this type, including the Carson City issues of 1871 and 1872 and a unique 1873-CC dime without arrows. In the case of the latter, although Mint records indicate that some 12,400 were struck, only one is known to exist, having been traced to once having been in the possession of Mint Director Snowden.

All of the Philadelphia dates from 1863 through 1867 were low mintage and are scarce in all grades. By contrast, San Francisco mintages of the dime were high during the same period. For example, in 1867, while the Philadelphia Mint struck a mere 6,625 dimes, the San Francisco facility coined some 140,000.

Arrows at date (1873-1874)

Designer: Christian Gobrecht. Size: 17.90 mm. Weight: 2.50 g. Composition: 90 percent silver (.0724 oz.), 10 percent copper.

As part of the Coinage Act of 1873, later dubbed the "Crime of 1873," attempts were made to adjust minor silver coinage to a metric standard. International monetary schemes, whereby standard weights in grams would be employed, were in vogue at the time.

The weight of the dime was raised to 2.50 grams to place it on a metric standard. Arrows were added to the date area of dimes struck in 1873 and 1874 to mark the increase in weight.

The Carson City dates of this type are the rarest, with a mintage of just 18,791 in 1873 and 10,817 in 1874.

Arrows at date removed (1875-1891)

Designer: Christian Gobrecht. Size: 17.90 mm. Weight: 2.50 g. Composition: 90 percent silver (.0724 oz.), 10 percent copper. Note: On an 1876-CC doubled-obverse variety, doubling appears in the words "of America" in the legend.

In 1875, the arrows that had been placed by the date beginning in 1873 were dropped.

Mintages of dimes, even from the Carson City Mint, were heavy into 1878 when all minor coins took a beating with the passage of the Bland-Allison Act. This act, a minor victory for the forces of free silver, forced the Mint to turn its attention to striking a new silver dollar.

Coinage of the dime at the Carson City Mint, which had in the prior year stood at 7.7 million, fell to 200,000 in 1878. The coinage dropped even more dramatically from 1879 through 1881, with scant mintages of 15,100, 37,355 and 24,975, respectively, from the Philadelphia Mint and no dimes struck at the branch mints. These dates are scarce in all grades.

The 1885-S, with a mintage of 43,690, is also scarce in all grades.

BARBER (1892-1916)

Designer: Charles E. Barber. Size: 17.90 mm. Weight: 2.50 g. Composition: 90 percent silver (.0724 oz.), 10 percent copper.

Mint Chief Engraver Charles Barber's design of a capped Liberty head was placed on the dime in 1892. It was also placed on the quarter and half dollar that same year.

First-year mintages of Barber dimes were high, as the Philadelphia Mint churned out 12.121 million and the New Orleans and San Francisco facilities contributed 3.841 million and 990,710 respectively.

Although the 1895-O, with a mintage of 440,000, is the series' regular-issue key and scarce in all grades, the most famous Barber dime is the 1894-S, of which only 24 were struck in proof. Theories vary as to why only 24 dimes were struck at the San Francisco Mint.

Only about a dozen 1894-S dimes are known to exist today.

MERCURY (1916-1945)

Designer: Adolph A. Weinman. Size: 17.90 mm. Weight: 2.50 g. Composition: 90 percent silver (.0724 oz.), 10 percent copper.

In 1916, as part of a wave of coinage redesign inspired by President Theodore Roosevelt, the winged Liberty, or Mercury dime, as it is commonly known today, was introduced. This design remains one of the most popular of all U.S. coins.

This series includes the notable 20th century overdates, the 1942/1 and 1942/1-D.

The most famous date, however, is the 1916-D, which carries high premiums in all grades. It had the series' lowest mintage of 264,000. Also in demand, even in low grades, are the 1921 and 1921-D.

ROOSEVELT (1946 TO DATE)

Silver composition (1946-1964)

Designer: John R. Sinnock. Size: 17.90 mm. Weight: 2.50 g. Composition: 90 percent silver (.0724 oz.), 10 percent copper.

Released in honor of President Franklin D. Roosevelt, the Roosevelt dime continued the trend toward placing portraits of presidents and statesmen on U.S. coins. The cent, nickel and quarter had already abandoned representations of Liberty in favor of depictions of Abraham Lincoln, Thomas Jefferson and George Washington.

The half dollar would follow in 1948, with Benjamin Franklin. When the dollar coin was reintroduced in 1971, it featured Dwight D. Eisenhower.

The 1949-S Roosevelt dime, with a mintage of 13,510 million, is generally considered the series' key.

Clad composition (1965 to date)

Designer: John R. Sinnock. Size: 17.90 mm. Weight: 2.27 g. Composition: clad layers of 75 percent copper and 25 percent nickel bonded to a pure copper core.

Faced with rising silver prices and a coinage shortage, the Mint dropped silver from the dime in 1965, replacing it with a base-metal clad composition, featuring an inner core of 100 percent copper. In 1982, a portion of the mintage included dimes missing the "P" mintmark. These command a strong premium.

20
CENTS

20-CENT PIECE (1875-1878)

Designer: William Barber. Size: 22 mm. Weight: 5 g.
Composition: 90 percent silver (.1447 oz.), 10 percent copper.

One of the shortest-lived U.S. coin series, the 20-cent piece was ostensibly the brainchild of Nevada Senator John Percival Jones, friend of the silver-mining interests. Jones had argued for the 20-cent denomination to alleviate problems making change in the West, where a lack of coins often caused the purchaser to be shortchanged in transactions involving a quarter.

The 20-cent piece's weight of 5 grams, it was believed, would make it convenient as an international coin as well, fitting in with the other silver coins that had been adjusted to a metric standard in 1873. The size and resemblance of the 20-cent piece to the Seated Liberty quarter, however, led to confusion and brought about its elimination as a coinage denomination in 1878.

The first year of mintage was the largest, with 1.155 million struck at the San Francisco Mint, an additional 133,290 minted in Carson City and another 39,700 struck at the parent mint in Philadelphia.

After that, mintage of the 20-cent piece dropped sharply to 15,900 in 1876 in Philadelphia and 10,000 at Carson City. The latter is a great rarity, as most were melted at the Mint. Less than two dozen 1876-CC 20-cent pieces are believed to have escaped the melting pot.

Only proofs were struck in 1877 (350) and 1878 (600).

Unlike the dimes, quarters, half dollars and silver dollars of the period, the edge of the 20-cent piece was plain instead of reeded and the word "Liberty" was raised on the surface rather than recessed.

25
CENTS

DRAPED BUST (1796-1807)

Small-eagle reverse (1796)

Designer: Robert Scot. Size: 27.5 mm. Weight: 6.74 g.
Composition: 89.24 percent silver (.1935 oz.), 10.76 percent copper.

Even though it was authorized by the Coinage Act of 1792, coinage of the quarter dollar did not begin until four years later. Featured on this low-mintage (6,146) and rare one-year type was Robert Scot's Draped Bust design with small-eagle reverse. The design was already in use on the large cent, half dime, dime, half dollar and silver dollar.

Heraldic-eagle reverse (1804-1807)

Designer: Robert Scot. Size: 27.5 mm. Weight: 6.74 g.
Composition: 89.24 percent silver (.1935 oz.), 10.76 percent copper.

After a hiatus of eight years, coinage of the quarter dollar began again in 1804, this time with the heraldic-eagle reverse, and for the first time expressing the denomination, shown as "25C" on the reverse.

First-year coinage of the Draped Bust quarter with the heraldic eagle was a miniscule 6,738. Thereafter, mintages increased to 121,394, 206,124 and 220,643 for the 1805 through 1807 coinage. All of these dates carry significant premiums in all states of preservation, though not as high as the 1804.

CAPPED BUST (1815-1838)

Large size
(1815-1828)

Designer: John Reich. Size: 27 mm. Weight: 6.74 g. Competition: 89.24 percent silver (.1935 oz.), 10.76 percent copper. Note: Varieties of the 1819 strikes are distinguished by the size of the "9" in the date. Varieties of the 1820 strikes are distinguished by the size of the "0" in the date.

Coinage of the quarter dollar was often sporadic at the first Mint. No quarters were struck from 1808 through 1814. When the quarter dollar was reintroduced in 1815, it carried the Capped Bust design credited to John Reich.

Due to the necessity of preserving die steel, many overdates exist of this type.

One of the more interesting varieties is the "25 over 50 C," which appears on some 1822- and 1828-dated quarters. Apparently the engraver blundered by placing the wrong denomination on the die and then corrected his mistake. After being used in 1822, the same die was again employed in 1828, despite the obvious mistake.

Two great rarities of the series are the 1823/2 and the 1827/3. Of the former, less than two dozen are believed to exist out of an original mintage of more than 17,000. Of the 1827/3, less than 10 are traced in proof, with an additional dozen or so restrikes known, having been produced more than 30 years later from scrapped Mint dies.

Small size
(1831-1838)

Designer: William Kneass. Size: 24.30 mm. Weight: 6.74 g. Competition: 89.24 percent silver (.1935 oz.), 10.76 percent copper. Note: Varieties of the 1831 strikes are distinguished by the size of the lettering on the reverse.

Use of a close collar, introduced at the Mint in the late 1820s, created a smaller diameter quarter, down from 27 millimeters to 24.3 millimeters. Another readily noticeable change to the design was the introduction of a raised border and the removal of the motto "E Pluribus Unum" from above the eagle.

SEATED LIBERTY (1838-1891)

No motto (1838-1853)

Designer: Christian Gobrecht. Size: 24.30 mm. Weight: 6.68 g. Composition: 90 percent silver (.1934 oz.), 10 percent copper. Note: 1852 obverse dies were used to strike the 1853 "no arrows" variety, with the "2" being recut to form a "3."

The adoption of Christian Gobrecht's Seated Liberty design for the quarter dollar was part of an overall trend toward uniformity of design of all U.S. silver coins. In 1840, Robert Ball Hughes modified the design, including an extra fold of drapery from Liberty's left elbow.

The 1840-O is known in "no drapery" and "drapery" varieties. In 1842, the date size was enlarged and two rarities resulted: the 1842 "small date" in proof, of which only six specimens are known; and the 1842-O circulation issue, which is generally found in low grades. Also rare are the 1849-O, 1852-O and 1853 without arrows and rays.

Arrows at date, reverse rays (1853)

Designer: Christian Gobrecht. Size: 24.30 mm. Weight: 6.22 g.
Composition: 90 percent silver (.1800 oz.), 10 percent copper.

In 1853, the quarter dollar joined the half dime, dime and half dollar in sporting arrows next to the date to mark the reduction in weight resulting from the Act of 1853. The quarter dollar and half dollar also showed a glory of rays around the eagle on the reverse.

The silver dollar was the only silver coin unaffected by the change, as its weight remained at the 412.5-grain standard.

This, however, led to lower mintages of the silver dollar and its constant hoarding and melting.

A popular one-year type coin, the "arrows and rays" quarter, was struck at Philadelphia in a mintage of more than 15 million and at New Orleans with a mintage of more than 1.3 million.

An 1853/4 overdate is known.

Reverse rays removed (1854-1855)

Designer: Christian Gobrecht. Size: 24.30 mm. Weight: 6.22 g. Composition: 90 percent silver
(.1800 oz.), 10 percent copper. Note: An 1854-O "huge O" variety has an oversized mintmark.

In 1854, the rays were removed from the reverse design of the quarter, but the arrows remained, still signaling the reduction in weight of the quarter first implemented in 1853. The use of this design type continued through 1855, with the branch-mint issues of New Orleans (176,000) and San Francisco (396,400) being scarce.

1855 also marked the first year of mintage of the quarter dollar at San Francisco.

Arrows at date removed (1856-1865)

Designer: Christian Gobrecht. Size: 24.30 mm. Weight: 6.22 g. Composition: 90 percent silver (.1800 oz.), 10 percent copper.

In 1856, the arrows that had been placed on the quarter dollar in 1853 to denote a reduction in the coin's weight were removed from the date area. But the quarter dollar remained at the same weight as the 1853 through 1855 issues. Branch-mint issues of this type generally had the lowest mintages and bring the strongest premiums in all grades. The 1860-S and 1864-S are scarce.

After banks suspended specie payments late in 1860 (not to be restored until 1878) precious metals were hoarded. Production of all silver coins at the Philadelphia Mint suffered.

From a high of 7.368 million in 1858, coinage of quarter dollars at the parent mint plummeted to 59,300 by 1865, making later Philadelphia business strikes scarce.

Motto above eagle (1866-1873)

Designer: Christian Gobrecht. Size: 24.30 mm. Weight: 6.22 g. Composition: 90 percent silver (.1800 oz.), 10 percent copper. Note: 1873 "closed 3" and "open 3" varieties are known and are distinguished by the amount of space between the upper left and lower left serifs in the "3."

The addition of a religious motto to the nation's coinage was first suggested by Rev. M.R. Watkinson of Pennsylvania and, after experimentation with several variations, the motto "In God We Trust" was adopted. It first appeared on the 2-cent piece in 1864 and in 1866 on the quarter dollar, half dollar, silver dollar and gold denominations above the gold quarter eagle.

Included in this type are several low mintage issues of Carson City. The Nevada facility, located only a short distance from the silver-rich Comstock Lode, began striking quarter dollars in 1870. With a scant mintage of 8,340, the coin carries a high premium date in all grades. Also very scarce are the 1871 through 1873 "CC" dates. The 1873-CC, with a mintage of 4,000, is a classic rarity of which only a handful of specimens are known to exist.

High prices of silver following the Civil War also kept mintages generally well below 100,000 per year at the Philadelphia and San Francisco mints throughout the first five years of issuance of this type. The 1866, with a mintage of 17,525, is a high-priced rarity, as are the 1871-S and 1872-S coins.

Arrows at date (1873-1874)

Designer: Christian Gobrecht. Size: 24.30 mm. Weight: 6.25 g.
Composition: 90 percent silver (.1808 oz.), 10 percent copper.

The Coinage Act of 1873, the first major overhaul of the nation's Mint laws since 1792, increased the weight of the quarter dollar from 6.22 to 6.25 grams. The move was motivated by a prevalent talk of international coinage based on the metric system and had the support of several influential people, including John Jay Knox, a framer of the Coinage Act of 1873.

Although mintage was more than 1.2 million at the Philadelphia Mint during 1873, the Carson City Mint struck only 12,462 quarter dollars, making the 1873-CC "arrows" quarter dollar rare.

Arrows at date removed (1875-1891)

Designer: Christian Gobrecht. Size: 24.30 mm. Weight: 6.25 g. Composition: 90 percent silver (.1808 oz.), 10 percent copper.

In 1875, the arrows that marked the quarter dollar's weight increase in 1873 were removed from the design.

Mintages at the Philadelphia Mint were high, reaching 17.817 million in 1876 and continuing strong until 1879, when the Bland-Allison Act, passed the year prior, forced the Mint to turn its attention to the production of silver dollars. From a mintage of 2.26 million in 1878, coinage at the Philadelphia facility dropped to 14,700 in 1879 and hovered in that range or lower until 1891, the last year of the Seated Liberty design.

BARBER (1892-1916)

Designer: Charles E. Barber. Size: 24.30 mm. Weight: 6.25 g. Composition: 90 percent silver (.1809 oz.), 10 percent copper.

Charles Barber's capped Liberty replaced the Seated Liberty design in 1892. A heraldic eagle occupied the reverse.

The Barber quarter was struck at the Philadelphia, New Orleans and San Francisco mints. Key dates include the 1896-S (188,039 minted), 1901-S (72,664 minted) and 1913-S (40,000 minted).

STANDING LIBERTY (1916-1930)

Type 1
(1916-1917)

Designer: Hermon A. MacNeil. Size: 24.30 mm. Weight: 6.25 g. Composition: 90 percent silver (.1809 oz.), 10 percent copper.

Hermon A. MacNeil, a noted sculptor, was a winner of a design competition that saw the introduction of new designs for the quarter.

MacNeil's design of a standing Liberty with shield raised in defense made its way onto the quarter in 1916.

Long-held belief has it that public outcry against the partial nudity of the design led to a modification covering Liberty's breast in early 1917. Letters written by MacNeil, however, suggest that in the end it was the artist who favored the design change and convinced the Mint to issue a redesigned coin.

Striking problems were prevalent through much of this series, and many dates are notorious for being weakly struck, especially in the design detail of Liberty's head.

The 1916, with a mintage of 52,000, is rare in all grades.

Type 2
(1917-1924)

Designer: Hermon A. MacNeil. Size: 24.30 mm. Weight: 6.25 g.
Composition: 90 percent silver (.1809 oz.), 10 percent copper.

Beginning in 1917, the design of the quarter was changed to include a chain-mail covering over Liberty's exposed right breast, which had appeared on all of the 1916 and some 1917 quarter dollars.

This design type includes the 1918/7-S overdate, one of the most dramatic in a limited number of 20th century overdates. The 1923-S is a key in all grades and rare with fully struck head detail. No quarters were minted in 1922.

Recessed date
(1925-1930)

Designer: Hermon A. MacNeil. Size: 24.30 mm. Weight: 6.25 g.
Composition: 90 percent silver (.1809 oz.), 10 percent copper.

From the outset of coinage of the Standing Liberty quarter dollar, one of the major problems with the design was the positioning of the date on a raised level. In 1925, the design was modified to place the date in recess to protect it from wear.

The 1926-S is a notable rarity with full head detail, as is the 1930-S. The 1927-S, with a mintage of 396,000, is a key date.

WASHINGTON (1932 TO DATE)

Silver composition
(1932-1964)

Designer: John Flanagan. Size: 24.30 mm. Weight: 6.25 g.
Composition: 90 percent silver (.1809 oz.), 10 percent copper.

The bicentennial of President George Washington's birth was the motivation behind the introduction of the Washington quarter in 1932. A judging commission selected a design by sculptor Laura Gardin Fraser, wife of Buffalo nickel designer James Earle Fraser. However, Treasury Secretary Andrew Mellon went with John Flanagan's design, based on Houdon's bust of the President.

The 1932-D and -S strikes are keys. Other dates have proven elusive in gem uncirculated condition.

Varieties include the 1934 light- and heavy-motto pieces, 1934 doubled die obverse, 1943-S doubled-die obverse, and two curious overmintmark pieces — the 1950-D/S and 1950-S/D.

Clad composition
(1965-1974)

Designer: John Flanagan. Size: 24.30 mm. Weight: 5.67 g. Composition: clad layers of 75 percent copper and 25 percent nickel bonded to a 100 percent copper core.

In 1965, silver was removed from all circulating coins, with the exception of the half dollar. Replacing the former 90 percent silver, 10 percent copper composition was a new sandwich metal, comprised of outer layers of 75 percent copper and 25 percent nickel and an inner core of 100 percent copper.

The Coinage Act of 1965 also discontinued the use of mintmarks, which were not restored to coinage until 1968. After 1968, the mintmark position was moved from the reverse of the quarter to the obverse.

Bicentennial reverse
(1975-1976)

Designer: John Flanagan, obverse; Jack L. Ahr, reverse. Size: 24.30 mm. Weight: 5.67 g. Composition: clad layers of 75 percent copper and 25 percent nickel bonded to a 100 percent copper core.

The U.S. Bicentennial celebration resulted in the creation of new designs for the reverse of the quarter, half dollar and Eisenhower dollar. An open design competition was held, and Jack L. Ahr's depiction of a Colonial drummer boy was selected for the quarter dollar.

Struck in 1975 and 1976, Bicentennial quarter dollars bear the distinctive dating "1776-1976."

Eagle reverse resumes
(1977-1998)

Designer: John Flanagan. Size: 24.30 mm. Weight: 5.67 g. Composition: clad layers of 75 percent copper and 25 percent nickel bonded to a 100 percent copper core.

The eagle returned to the quarter dollar in 1977, in a slightly lower relief. It would remain there until 1999, when the Mint introduced its 50 State Quarter Program, honoring each of the nation's states with its own coin.

50 States, Delaware (1999)

Size: 24.30 mm. Weight: 5.67 g. Composition: clad layers of 75 percent copper and 25 percent nickel bonded to a 100 percent copper core.

In 1999, the U.S. Mint produced quarters with special reverse designs honoring Delaware, Pennsylvania, New Jersey, Georgia and Connecticut, the first five states to enter the Union. Designs were selected in various manners, including competitions within the state being honored. The program called for the release of five new reverse designs each year, in order of the state's entry into the Union. Delaware's coin showed Caesar Rodney's famous ride to Independence Hall in Philadelphia to cast the deciding vote in favor of the nation's independence from Great Britain. Delaware joined the Union in 1787, as reflected on the coin.

50 States, Pennsylvania (1999)

Size: 24.30 mm. Weight: 5.67 g. Composition: clad layers of 75 percent copper and 25 percent nickel bonded to a 100 percent copper core.

The statue, "Commonwealth," from Pennsylvania's state capitol dome in Harrisburg, Pa., is displayed over the state outline. The state motto, "Virtue/ Liberty/Independence," also appears on Pennsylvania's 1999 quarter. Commonwealth holds a mace in her left arm, symbolizing justice. A keystone is also shown, relating to the state's nickname of "The Keystone State." Pennsylvania became a state in 1787.

50 States, New Jersey
(1999)

Size: 24.30 mm. Weight: 5.67 g. Composition: clad layers of 75 percent copper and 25 percent nickel bonded to a 100 percent copper core.

Gen. George Washington and the Colonial Army crossed the Delaware on New Jersey's 1999 quarter. The scene was based on Emmanuel Leutze's painting, "Washington Crossing the Delaware," and depicted the Christmas night 1776 crossing into Trenton, N.J. Washington and members of the Colonial Army took the British by surprise, marking a turning point in the Revolutionary War. New Jersey joined the Union in 1787.

50 States, Georgia
(1999)

Size: 24.30 mm. Weight: 5.67 g. Composition: clad layers of 75 percent copper and 25 percent nickel bonded to a 100 percent copper core.

The Georgia peach served as the central design on this state's 1999 quarter. It was surrounded by the outline of the state and live oak sprigs. "Wisdom, Justice, Moderation," the state motto, appeared on a banner. Georgia entered the Union in 1788.

50 States, Connecticut
(1999)

Size: 24.30 mm. Weight: 5.67 g. Composition: clad layers of 75 percent copper and 25 percent nickel bonded to a 100 percent copper core.

The historic Charter Oak dominated Connecticut's 1999 quarter. The famed white oak tree, which no longer exists, served as the hiding place for the state charter, which had been saved from the British, in 1687, by Capt. Joseph Wadsworth. The tree fell in a storm in 1856. Connecticut entered the Union in 1788.

50 States, Massachusetts
(2000)

Size: 24.30 mm. Weight: 5.67 g. Composition: clad layers of 75 percent copper and 25 percent nickel bonded to a 100 percent copper core.

An ever vigilant Minuteman, based on a statue at The Minuteman National Historical Park in Concord, Mass., appeared above the state outline on Massachusetts' 2000 quarter. The Minutemen helped defeat the British in the Revolutionary War. Massachusetts, also known as "The Bay State," entered the Union in 1788.

50 States, Maryland
(2000)

Size: 24.30 mm. Weight: 5.67 g. Composition: clad layers of 75 percent copper and 25 percent nickel bonded to a 100 percent copper core.

The wooden dome of the Maryland Statehouse, flanked by sprigs of white oak (the state tree), graced "The Old Line State" quarter design for 2000. The Treaty of Paris, officially ending the Revolutionary War, was ratified in the statehouse. Maryland entered the Union in 1788.

50 States, South Carolina
(2000)

Size: 24.30 mm. Weight: 5.67 g. Composition: clad layers of 75 percent copper and 25 percent nickel bonded to a 100 percent copper core.

A palmetto tree, the Carolina wren and the state flower, the yellow jessamine, appeared with the state outline on the 2000 South Carolina coin. Known as the Palmetto State, after colonists built a fort out of palmetto logs and defeated a British fleet attempting to take Charleston Harbor, South Carolina joined the Union in 1788.

50 States, New Hampshire
(2000)

Size: 24.30 mm. Weight: 5.67 g. Composition: clad layers of 75 percent copper and 25 percent nickel bonded to a 100 percent copper core.

New Hampshire's famous 40-foot-tall landmark, the Old Man of the Mountain, was shown on the New Hampshire coin for 2000. The rock formation on Mt. Cannon in the Franconia Notch unfortunately collapsed in 2003. The quarter also bore the state motto, "Live Free or Die." New Hampshire joined the Union in 1788 as the ninth state.

50 States, Virginia
(2000)

Size: 24.30 mm. Weight: 5.67 g. Composition: clad layers of 75 percent copper and 25 percent nickel bonded to a 100 percent copper core.

The 1606 expedition of the Virginia Company to colonize the New World was marked on Virginia's 2000 quarter by depictions of the three ships that took part in the expedition: the *Susan Constant*, *Godspeed* and *Discovery*. In May 1607, they landed on an island along the James River, which would become the site of Jamestown, the first permanent English settlement. Virginia joined the Union in 1788.

50 States, New York
(2001)

Size: 24.30 mm. Weight: 5.67 g. Composition: clad layers of 75 percent copper and 25 percent nickel bonded to a 100 percent copper core.

New York, hailed as the "Gateway to Freedom" because of its great role in immigration, was honored on a 2001 quarter showing the Statue of Liberty before an outline of the state that also shows a line depicting the Hudson River and the route of the Erie Canal. It also has 11 stars for the number of states when New York entered the Union, in 1788.

50 States, North Carolina
(2001)

Size: 24.30 mm. Weight: 5.67 g. Composition: clad layers of 75 percent copper and 25 percent nickel bonded to a 100 percent copper core.

The first successful powered aircraft flight, as recreated from a 1903 photograph taken at Kitty Hawk, N.C., on Dec. 17, 1903, marked the North Carolina quarter for 2001. On Dec. 17, Orville Wright was at the controls as the Flyer I traveled 120 feet. North Carolina entered the Union in 1789.

50 States, Rhode Island
(2001)

Size: 24.30 mm. Weight: 5.67 g. Composition: clad layers of 75 percent copper and 25 percent nickel bonded to a 100 percent copper core.

A sailboat on Narragansett Bay, with a depiction of Pell Bridge in the background, was featured on "The Ocean State" quarter from Rhode Island. Rhode Island has long been home to the America's Cup sailing competition. Rhode Island joined the Union in 1790.

50 States, Vermont
(2001)

Size: 24.30 mm. Weight: 5.67 g. Composition: clad layers of 75 percent copper and 25 percent nickel bonded to a 100 percent copper core.

Vermont's production of maple syrup was honored on the state's 2001 quarter, with Camel's Hump Mountain in the background as sap is being collected from maple trees in the foreground. The motto, "Freedom and Unity," also appeared. Vermont was admitted to the Union in 1791.

50 States, Kentucky
(2001)

Size: 24.30 mm. Weight: 5.67 g. Composition: clad layers of 75 percent copper and 25 percent nickel bonded to a 100 percent copper core.

The 2001 quarter from Kentucky featured Federal Hill, where Stephen Foster wrote the state song, "My Old Kentucky Home." A thoroughbred racehorse is in the foreground with the inscription 'My Old Kentucky Home" above. Kentucky, which joined the Union in 1792, is home to the Kentucky Derby.

50 States, Tennessee
(2002)

Size: 24.30 mm. Weight: 5.67 g. Composition: clad layers of 75 percent copper and 25 percent nickel bonded to a 100 percent copper core.

Tennessee's "Musical Heritage" was celebrated on its 2002 quarter, which shows a fiddle, representing the Appalachian music of east Tennessee, a trumpet for the blues of west Tennessee, home to Memphis, and a guitar for central Tennessee, home to Nashville. Three stars on the coin represented these regions. Tennessee joined the Union in 1796.

50 States, Ohio
(2002)

Size: 24.30 mm. Weight: 5.67 g. Composition: clad layers of 75 percent copper and 25 percent nickel bonded to a 100 percent copper core.

Heralding its role as the "Birthplace of Aviation Pioneers," Ohio celebrated with a state quarter in 2002. It showed a biplane and an astronaut over an outline of the state. Ohio was the birthplace to Neil Armstrong and John Glenn, as well as Orville Wright. Orville and Wilbur Wright also tested one of their early aircraft, the 1905 Flyer III, in Ohio. Ohio became a state in 1803.

50 States, Louisiana
(2002)

Size: 24.30 mm. Weight: 5.67 g. Composition: clad layers of 75 percent copper and 25 percent nickel bonded to a 100 percent copper core.

The Louisiana Purchase was celebrated on Louisiana's 2002 quarter along with the state bird, the pelican, and a trumpet with musical notes, representing Louisiana's musical heritage rooted in jazz. An outline of the land purchased by Thomas Jefferson from Napoleon Bonaparte on a map of the United States showed the 13 new states added by the 1803 $15 million purchase. Louisiana became a state in 1812.

50 States, Indiana
(2002)

Size: 24.30 mm. Weight: 5.67 g. Composition: clad layers of 75 percent copper and 25 percent nickel bonded to a 100 percent copper core.

Home to the famed Indianapolis 500 auto race, Indiana marked its 2002 quarter with an Indy 500 car over the state outline and the legend "Crossroads of America." A circle of 19 stars signified Indiana as the 19th state. It joined the Union in 1816.

50 States, Mississippi
(2002)

Size: 24.30 mm. Weight: 5.67 g. Composition: clad layers of 75 percent copper and 25 percent nickel bonded to a 100 percent copper core.

Mississippi represented itself as "The Magnolia State" on its 2002 quarter. It showed the leaves and blossoms of the state flower, the magnolia. Mississippi became a state in 1817.

50 States, Illinois
(2003)

Size: 24.30 mm. Weight: 5.67 g. Composition: clad layers of 75 percent copper and 25 percent nickel bonded to a 100 percent copper core.

Fittingly, Abraham Lincoln dominated the state outline on the 2003 Illinois quarter. The state, which served as the birthplace to the nation's 16th president, is known as the "Land of Lincoln." The coin was bordered by 21 stars, marking the state's place as the 21st to join the Union. It became a state in 1818.

50 States, Alabama
(2003)

Size: 24.30 mm. Weight: 5.67 g. Composition: clad layers of 75 percent copper and 25 percent nickel bonded to a 100 percent copper core.

Helen Keller, reading a book in Braille, graced the reverse of Alabama's quarter. Her name also appeared on the coin in Braille. Keller was born in Alabama in 1880, and lost her sight and hearing as a child. A "Spirit of Courage" banner is above the date and reflected Keller's accomplishments, despite her disabilities. Alabama was the 22nd state to enter the Union. It did so in December 1819.

50 States, Maine
(2003)

Size: 24.30 mm. Weight: 5.67 g. Composition: clad layers of 75 percent copper and 25 percent nickel bonded to a 100 percent copper core.

On Maine's quarter, the Pemaquid Point Light, in New Harbor, Maine, illuminated the way for a schooner at sea, protecting it in an area known for its shipwrecks. Funds for the lighthouse were granted by Congress in 1826. Maine became a state in 1820.

50 States, Missouri
(2003)

Size: 24.30 mm. Weight: 5.67 g. Composition: clad layers of 75 percent copper and 25 percent nickel bonded to a 100 percent copper core.

On the Missouri quarter, famed explorers Lewis and Clark were shown paddling toward St. Louis via Missouri River, with the Jefferson National Expansion Memorial (Gateway Arch) in the background. The explorers arrived in the city in 1806, ending their historic journey westward and back that began in St. Charles, Mo., in 1804. The inscription, "Corps of Discovery 1804-2004," is above and surrounding the Gateway Arch. Missouri became a state in 1821.

50 States, Arkansas
(2003)

Size: 24.30 mm. Weight: 5.67 g. Composition: clad layers of 75 percent copper and 25 percent nickel bonded to a 100 percent copper core.

A mixture of images representing Arkansas's natural resources graced the Arkansas quarter of 2003. Shown were rice stalks, a diamond and a mallard flying above a lake. Besides it many natural lakes and its hunting opportunities, Arkansas is home to Crater of Diamonds State Park, where visitors can hunt for and keep any diamonds they find. Arkansas entered the Union in 1836.

50 States, Michigan
(2004)

Size: 24.30 mm. Weight: 5.67 g. Composition: clad layers of 75 percent copper and 25 percent nickel bonded to a 100 percent copper core.

Michigan's nickname, the "Great Lakes State," was marked by its 2004 quarter, which showed the Great Lakes – Superior, Michigan, Huron, Erie and Ontario – bordering the state. Michigan entered the Union in 1837 as the 26th state.

50 States, Florida
(2004)

Size: 24.30 mm. Weight: 5.67 g. Composition: clad layers of 75 percent copper and 25 percent nickel bonded to a 100 percent copper core.

Announcing itself as the "Gateway to Discovery," Florida's 2004 quarter contrasted a 16th century Spanish galleon, a space shuttle and land with sabal palm trees. The Spanish galleon reflected the various voyages of discovery, including those of Ponce de Leon, who, according to the U.S. Mint's description of the coinage design, visited during Easter 1513 while searching for the Fountain of Youth. He named the region "Pascua Florida" ("Flowery Easter"). Florida is also home to the Kennedy Space Center. Florida entered the Union in 1845.

50 States, Texas
(2004)

Size: 24.30 mm. Weight: 5.67 g. Composition: clad layers of 75 percent copper and 25 percent nickel bonded to a 100 percent copper core.

Texas, "The Lone Star State," placed a star over a topographical map of the state. A lariat, representing the state's cowboy history, encircles the design. Texas added its star to the map in 1845.

50 States, Iowa
(2004)

Size: 24.30 mm. Weight: 5.67 g. Composition: clad layers of 75 percent copper and 25 percent nickel bonded to a 100 percent copper core.

A painting by Iowan Grant Wood, "Arbor Day," was used as the basis for Iowa's 2004 quarter design, along with the inscription, "Foundation in Education," reflecting the state's commitment to small-town values and education. Iowa became a state in 1846.

50 States, Wisconsin
(2004)

Size: 24.30 mm. Weight: 5.67 g. Composition: clad layers of 75 percent copper and 25 percent nickel bonded to a 100 percent copper core.

The state's dairy industry was celebrated on the 2004 Wisconsin quarter, which showed a cow and a head of cheese. Also shown was an ear of corn and the state motto, "Forward." Wisconsin joined the Union in 1848.

50 States, California
(2005)

Size: 24.30 mm. Weight: 5.67 g. Composition: clad layers of 75 percent copper and 25 percent nickel bonded to a 100 percent copper core.

Conservationist John Muir was shown admiring Yosemite Valley's granite "Half Dome" on the 2005 California quarter. The once nearly extinct California condor is also shown in flight. As president of the Sierra Club, Muir helped protect Yosemite National Park, established by Congress in 1890. California entered the Union in 1850, shortly after the great gold rush began.

50 States, Minnesota
(2005)

Size: 24.30 mm. Weight: 5.67 g. Composition: clad layers of 75 percent copper and 25 percent nickel bonded to a 100 percent copper core.

Touting its many lakes with its nickname, "Land of 10,000 Lakes," appearing over the state outline, Minnesota's 2005 quarter also showed a loon and two people fishing before a shoreline of trees. Minnesota entered the Union in 1858.

50 States, Oregon
(2005)

Size: 24.30 mm. Weight: 5.67 g. Composition: clad layers of 75 percent copper and 25 percent nickel bonded to a 100 percent copper core.

Known for being the deepest lake in the United States, some 1,949 feet in depth, Crater Lake was shown on Oregon's 2005 quarter. The coin also showed Wizard Island, the Watchman and Hillman peaks, and a line of conifers. Crater Lake National Park, established in 1902 by President Theodore Roosevelt, is the sixth oldest national park in the nation. Oregon joined the Union in 1859.

50 States, Kansas
(2005)

Size: 24.30 mm. Weight: 5.67 g. Composition: clad layers of 75 percent copper and 25 percent nickel bonded to a 100 percent copper core.

A bison and a sunflower, both state symbols, graced the 2005 quarter from Kansas. In 1861, Kansas became the 34th state to join the Union.

50 States, West Virginia
(2005)

Size: 24.30 mm. Weight: 5.67 g. Composition: clad layers of 75 percent copper and 25 percent nickel bonded to a 100 percent copper core.

New River and the New River Gorge Bridge were shown on West Virginia's 2005 quarter. The bridge, an engineering wonder, is the world's largest steel span and the second highest bridge in the United States. West Virginia, known as the "Mountain State," joined the Union in 1863.

50 States, Nevada
(2006)

Size: 24.30 mm. Weight: 5.67 g. Composition: clad layers of 75 percent copper and 25 percent nickel bonded to a 100 percent copper core.

Three wild mustangs, typifying the state's large population of wild horses, were shown before snow-capped mountains and the sun on Nevada's 2006 quarter. Known as the "Silver State" for its rich deposits of silver ore, which include the famed Comstock Lode, Nevada was admitted to the Union in 1864.

50 States, Nebraska
(2006)

Size: 24.30 mm. Weight: 5.67 g. Composition: clad layers of 75 percent copper and 25 percent nickel bonded to a 100 percent copper core.

On Nebraska's quarter, a family was shown heading west aboard an ox-drawn covered wagon, passing by landmark Chimney Rock, on their way to a new life. The sun is in view in the background of this coin. Nebraska entered the Union in 1867.

50 States, Colorado
(2006)

Size: 24.30 mm. Weight: 5.67 g. Composition: clad layers of 75 percent copper and 25 percent nickel bonded to a 100 percent copper core.

The Rocky Mountains were celebrated on the 2006 Colorado quarter, which also bears evergreen trees and a banner with the inscription, "Colorful Colorado." Colorado joined the Union in 1876 as the 38th state.

50 States, North Dakota
(2006)

Size: 24.30 mm. Weight: 5.67 g. Composition: clad layers of 75 percent copper and 25 percent nickel bonded to a 100 percent copper core.

In a view typifying North Dakota and its Badlands, two bison were shown grazing before a sunset in North Dakota's Badlands region, with its buttes and canyons, on the 2006 North Dakota quarter. North Dakota entered the Union in 1889.

50 States, South Dakota
(2006)

Size: 24.30 mm. Weight: 5.67 g. Composition: clad layers of 75 percent copper and 25 percent nickel bonded to a 100 percent copper core.

South Dakota's famed landmark, Mount Rushmore, with a Chinese ring-necked pheasant, the state bird, in flight overhead graced South Dakota's 2006 quarter. Also shown were two heads of wheat. Mount Rushmore, which depicts George Washington, Thomas Jefferson, Theodore Roosevelt and Abraham Lincoln, was sculpted by Gutzon Borglum. Borglum was also responsible for the carving of Stone Mountain in Georgia and for the Stone Mountain commemorative half dollar. South Dakota joined the Union in 1889.

50 States, Montana
(2007)

Size: 24.30 mm. Weight: 5.67 g. Composition: clad layers of 75 percent copper and 25 percent nickel bonded to a 100 percent copper core.

The skull of a bison loomed over a landscape scene on Montana's 2007 quarter. Montana is known as "Big Sky Country," which is also represented by an inscription on the coin. Montana became the 41st state in 1889.

50 States, Washington
(2007)

Size: 24.30 mm. Weight: 5.67 g. Composition: clad layers of 75 percent copper and 25 percent nickel bonded to a 100 percent copper core.

A king salmon breached the water in front of Mount Rainier, an active volcano, on Washington's 2007 quarter. Known as "The Evergreen State," Washington joined the Union in 1889.

50 States, Idaho
(2007)

Size: 24.30 mm. Weight: 5.67 g. Composition: clad layers of 75 percent copper and 25 percent nickel bonded to a 100 percent copper core.

A peregrine falcon loomed over an outline of the state on Idaho's 2007 quarter, which also carried the state motto, "Esto Perpetua" ("May it be Forever"). Once an endangered specie, the peregrine falcon is known for its speed of flight. Idaho entered the Union in 1890.

50 States, Wyoming
(2007)

Size: 24.30 mm. Weight: 5.67 g. Composition: clad layers of 75 percent copper and 25 percent nickel bonded to a 100 percent copper core.

Wyoming, nicknamed the "Equality State," featured a bucking horse and rider on its 2007 quarter to mark its Wild West heritage. Wyoming gained the nickname, "Equality State," after its role in establishing equal voting rights for women and being the first state to grant "female suffrage." Wyoming became a state in 1890.

50 States, Utah
(2007)

Size: 24.30 mm. Weight: 5.67 g. Composition: clad layers of 75 percent copper and 25 percent nickel bonded to a 100 percent copper core.

Recreating the famous 1869 joining of the Central Pacific and Union Pacific railroads at Promontory Point, Utah, the Utah quarter showed two locomotives facing each other, with the final spike between. The legend, "Crossroads of the West," was also shown. Utah joined the Union in 1896.

50 States, Oklahoma
(2008)

Size: 24.30 mm. Weight: 5.67 g. Composition: clad layers of 75 percent copper and 25 percent nickel bonded to a 100 percent copper core.

The state bird, the scissortail flycatcher, was shown in flight on Oklahoma's 2008 quarter. Also shown was the state flower, the Indian blanket, and other wildflowers. Oklahoma became a state in 1907.

50 States, New Mexico
(2008)

Size: 24.30 mm. Weight: 5.67 g. Composition: clad layers of 75 percent copper and 25 percent nickel bonded to a 100 percent copper core.

A Zia sun symbol appeared over a topographical outline of the state on New Mexico's quarter, reflecting the impact of Native American culture on the state, including the Zia Pueblo. New Mexico, known as the "Land of Enchantment," was the 47th state. It was admitted to the Union in 1912.

50 States, Arizona
(2008)

Size: 24.30 mm. Weight: 5.67 g. Composition: clad layers of 75 percent copper and 25 percent nickel bonded to a 100 percent copper core.

An image of the Grand Canyon dominated Arizona's 2008 quarter. Also shown were a saguaro cactus and a banner reading "Grand Canyon State." A natural wonder, the Grand Canyon covers much of northwestern Arizona. Arizona entered the Union in 1912 and that date also appeared on the coin.

50 States, Alaska
(2008)

Size: 24.30 mm. Weight: 5.67 g. Composition: clad layers of 75 percent copper and 25 percent nickel bonded to a 100 percent copper core.

Featuring a grizzly bear with a salmon in its mouth, the reverse of the 2008 Alaska quarter was selected from more than 850 design submissions. According to fact sheets prepared by the U.S. Mint, the word "Alaska" comes from an Aleutian word "Alyeska," meaning "The Great Land." In 1959, Alaska became the 49th state admitted to the Union.

50 States, Hawaii
(2008)

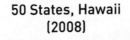

Size: 24.30 mm. Weight: 5.67 g. Composition: clad layers of 75 percent copper and 25 percent nickel bonded to a 100 percent copper core.

Hawaii, the last state honored, featured Kamehameha I, the first king of Hawaii. The state's motto, "Ua Mau ke Ea o ka 'ina i ka Pono," ("The Life of the Land is Perpetuated in Righteousness") is also shown. Hawaii entered the Union in 1959 as the 50th state.

District of Columbia and U.S. Territories, District of Columbia (2009)

Designer: John Flanagan, obverse; Joel Iskowitz, Don Everhart, reverse. Size: 24.30 mm. Weight: 5.67 g. Composition: clad layers of 75 percent copper and 25 percent nickel bonded to a 100 percent copper core.

Legendary composer and musician Edward Kennedy "Duke" Ellington appeared on the first of the District of Columbia and U.S. Territories quarters, which followed the 50 states coins. Also shown is D.C.'s Latin motto, "Justitia Omnibus" ("Justice for All"). The District of Columbia was created in 1790 and became the nation's capital in 1800.

District of Columbia and U.S. Territories, Puerto Rico (2009)

Designer: John Flanagan, obverse; Joseph Menna, reverse. Size: 24.30 mm. Weight: 5.67 g. Composition: clad layers of 75 percent copper and 25 percent nickel bonded to a 100 percent copper core.

A sentry box built into the massive stone walls surrounding and protecting the capital of San Juan was a major focal point of Puerto Rico's 2009 quarter. The island was ceded to the United States in 1898 from Spain, which had ruled it for hundreds of years. Also shown was a hibiscus flower and the island's motto, "Isla del Encanto" ("Isle of Enchantment").

District of Columbia and U.S. Territories, Guam (2009)

Designer: John Flanagan, obverse; James Licaretz, reverse. Size: 24.30 mm. Weight: 5.67 g. Composition: clad layers of 75 percent copper and 25 percent nickel bonded to a 100 percent copper core.

A topographical map of the island appeared along with a latte and a flying proa on Guam's 2009 quarter. A latte is a goblet-shaped stone used to hold buildings up, and the flying proa is a type of canoe with a sail. Long ruled by the Spanish, the people of Guam gained U.S. citizenship in 1950.

District of Columbia and U.S. Territories, American Samoa (2009)

Designer: John Flanagan, obverse; Charles Vickers, reverse. Size: 24.30 mm. Weight: 5.67 g. Composition: clad layers of 75 percent copper and 25 percent nickel bonded to a 100 percent copper core.

Featured on the American Samoa quarter was an ava bowl, a fly whisk and a staff. All of these items appear on American Somoa's official seal and are used in special ceremonies for island chiefs and their guests. American Samoa became a territory of the United States in 1929. Also shown were a coconut tree on the coastline and the motto, "Samoa Muamua Le Atua" ("Samoa, God is First").

District of Columbia and U.S. Territories, U.S. Virgin Islands (2009)

Designer: John Flanagan, obverse; Joseph Menna, reverse. Size: 24.30 mm. Weight: 5.67 g. Composition: clad layers of 75 percent copper and 25 percent nickel bonded to a 100 percent copper core.

The yellow breast, or banana quit, the official bird of the U.S. Virgin Islands, along with the yellow cedar or yellow elder, the official flower, and the tyre palm, the official tree, graced this coin and reflect the islands' role as a major tourist destination. The main islands and inlets that make up the U.S. Virgin Islands were first acquired by the United States from Denmark in 1917. In 1927, residents became U.S. citizens. Also shown is the outline of the three major islands, St. Croix, St. Thomas and St. John, along with the motto "United in Pride and Hope."

District of Columbia and U.S. Territories, Northern Mariana Islands (2009)

Designer: John Flanagan, obverse; Phebe Hemphill, reverse. Size: 24.30 mm. Weight: 5.67 g. Composition: clad layers of 75 percent copper and 25 percent nickel bonded to a 100 percent copper core.

The final coin in the District of Columbia and U.S. Territories program honored the Northern Mariana Islands, which became a commonwealth in

1975. Shown were a latte (used to support buildings in ancient times), a canoe, two white fairy terns flying overhead and a string of flowers worn around the head (known as a "mwar," and a symbol of honor and respect).

America the Beautiful
(2010-2021)

Designer: John Flanagan, obverse; various designers, reverses. Size: 24.30 mm. Weight: 5.67 g. Composition: clad layers of 75 percent copper and 25 percent nickel bonded to a 100 percent copper core.

In 2010 the U.S. Mint began the release of new quarter designs featuring depictions of national parks and other national sites to be issued five per year in the order in which they became a national site. Following is the listing of themes into 2021.

2010

Arkansas, Hot Springs National Park; Wyoming, Yellowstone National Park; California, Yosemite National Park; Arizona, Grand Canyon National; Oregon, Mt. Hood National Forest.

2011

Pennsylvania, Gettysburg National Military Park; Montana, Glacier National Park; Washington, Olympic National Park; Mississippi, Vicksburg National Military Park; Oklahoma, Chickasaw National Recreation Area.

2012

Puerto Rico, El Yunque National Forest; New Mexico, Chaco Culture National Historical Park; Maine, Acadia National Park; Hawaii, Hawai'i Volcanoes National Park; Alaska, Denali National Park.

2013

New Hampshire, White Mountain National Forest; Ohio, Perry's Victory and International Peace Memorial; Nevada, Great Basin National Park; Maryland, Fort McHenry National Monument and Historic Shrine; South Dakota, Mount Rushmore National Memorial.

2014

Tennessee, Great Smoky Mountains National Park; Virginia, Shenandoah National Park; Utah, Arches National Park; Colorado, Great Sand Dunes National Park; Florida, Everglades National Park.

2015

Nebraska, Homestead National Monument of America; Louisiana, Kisatchie National Forest; North Carolina, Blue Ridge Parkway; Delaware, Bombay Hook National Wildlife Refuge; New York, Saratoga National Historical Park.

2016

Illinois, Shawnee National Forest; Kentucky, Cumberland Gap National Historical Park; West Virginia, Harpers Ferry National Historical Park; North Dakota, Theodore Roosevelt National Park; South Carolina, Fort Moultrie (Fort Sumter National Monument).

2017

Iowa, Effigy Mounds National Monument; District of Columbia, Frederick Douglass National Historic Site; Missouri, Ozark National Scenic Riverways; New Jersey, Ellis Island National Monument (Statue of Liberty); Indiana, George Rogers Clark National Historical Park.

2018

Michigan, Pictured Rocks National Lakeshore; Wisconsin, Apostle Islands National Lakeshore; Minnesota, Voyageurs National Park; Georgia, Cumberland Island National Seashore; Rhode Island, Block Island National Wildlife Refuge.

2019

Massachusetts, Lowell National Historical Park; Northern Mariana Islands, American Memorial Park; Guam, War in the Pacific National Historical Park; Texas, San Antonio Missions National Historical Park; Idaho, Frank Church River of No Return Wilderness.

2020

American Samoa, National Park of American Samoa; Connecticut, Weir Farm National Historic Site; U.S. Virgin Islands, Salt River Bay National Historical Park and Ecological Preserve; Vermont, Marsh-Billings-Rockefeller National Historical Park; Kansas, Tallgrass Prairie National Preserve.

2021

Alabama, Tuskegee Airmen National Historic Site.

50
CENTS

FLOWING HAIR (1794-1795)

Designer: Robert Scot. Size: 32.50 mm. Weight: 13.48 g.
Composition: 89.24 percent silver (.3869 oz.), 10.76 percent copper.

Robert Scot's Flowing Hair design, with small-eagle reverse, graced the nation's first half dollar as it did the half dime and dollar. Minus the liberty cap and pole, the obverse design was much the same as that on the half cent and the large cent.

As the dies were largely engraved by hand, many varieties exist. Many pieces also exhibit adjustment (file) marks caused at the Mint as the overweight planchets were brought to the proper weight.

The 1794 is the scarcest date of this type, with 23,464 minted.

DRAPED BUST (1796-1807)

Small-eagle reverse
(1796-1797)

Designer: Robert Scot. Size: 32.50 mm. Weight: 13.48 g.
Composition: 89.24 percent silver (.3869 oz.), 10.76 percent copper.

With a combined mintage of under 4,000 for the 1796 and 1797 dates, the Draped Bust half dollar with small-eagle reverse is a true scarcity and accordingly priced even in the lowest grades. The design is credited to Mint Engraver Robert Scot and was based on a Gilbert Stuart drawing. Stuart is probably best known for his famed painting of George Washington.

The Draped Bust design, adopted in 1796 for use on all silver and copper coins except for the half cent, was employed through 1807 before giving way to designs by John Reich.

Heraldic-eagle reverse
(1801-1807)

Designer: Robert Scot. Size: 32.50 mm. Weight: 13.48 g. Composition: 89.24 percent silver (.3869 oz.), 10.76 percent copper. Note: Two varieties of the 1803 strikes are distinguished by the size of the "3" in the date. The several varieties of the 1806 strikes are distinguished by the style of "6" in the date, size of the stars on the obverse, and whether the stem of the olive branch held by the eagle extends through the claw.

When half dollar coinage resumed in 1801, Robert Scot's heraldic eagle had replaced the small eagle reverse used on the 1796 and 1797 half dollars.

Varieties are plentiful, including an 1805/4 overdate. This variety is especially interesting, as no half dollars were minted bearing an 1804 date.

Because of the high relief of the Draped Bust obverse, many of the dates of this type exhibit strike weakness on the reverse.

CAPPED BUST (1807-1839)

Lettered edge
(1807-1836)

Designer: John Reich. Size: 32.50 mm. Weight: 13.48 g. Composition: 89.24 percent silver (.3869 oz.), 10.76 percent copper. Note: Two varieties of the 1807 strikes are distinguished by the size of the stars on the obverse. Two varieties of the 1811 are distinguished by the size of the "8" in the date. A third has a period between the "8" and the second "1" in the date. One variety of the 1817 has a period between the "1" and the "7" in the date. Two varieties of the 1819/18 overdate are distinguished by the size of the "9" in the date. Two varieties of the 1820 are distinguished by the size of the date. On 1823 varieties, the "broken 3" appears to be almost separated in the middle of the "3" in the date; the "patched 3" has the error repaired; the "ugly 3" has portions of its detail missing. The 1827 "curled 2" and "square 2" varieties are distinguished by the numeral's base—either curled or square. Among the 1828 varieties, "knobbed 2" and "no knob" refers to whether the upper left serif of the digit is rounded. 1830 varieties are distinguished by the size of the "0" in the date. The four 1834 varieties are distinguished by the size of the stars, date and letters in the inscription. The 1836 "50/00" variety was struck from a reverse die that had "50" recut over "00" in the denomination.

John Reich's design appeared on the half dollar beginning in 1807, replacing Robert Scot's. Blundered dies and varieties are the rule in this type, not the exception. Much of the operations at the first Mint were done by hand and open to human error.

One of the more interesting varieties is the 1807 with "50," representing the denomination, punched over "20."

Some varieties involve slight differences while others are dramatic. In 1813, for example, an engraver placed the denomination "50C" over "Uni," apparently to correct improper positioning of the beginning of "United States." On an 1814 strike, an "E" had to be punched over the letter "A" in "States" to correct the spelling.

Scarce dates include the 1815/2 and 1817/4 strikes.

Reeded edge, '50 Cents' on reverse (1836-1837)

Designer: Christian Gobrecht. Size: 30 mm. Weight: 13.36 g.
Composition: 90 percent silver (.3867 oz.), 10 percent copper.

Adoption of a close collar in the late 1820s led to the use of a reeded edge on the half dollar in place of the lettered edge. Unlike the lettered edge, which had been applied before striking by a separate machine, reeding was applied during striking as the metal flowed into the collar.

The denomination now read "50 Cents," whereas on prior Capped Bust halves it had been represented as "50 C."

Mintage in 1836 of the reeded-edge half dollar was low, at slightly more than 1,000. Type collectors looking to save money may want to opt for the less expensive and more plentiful 1837 strike of which 3.6 million were minted.

'Half Dol.' on reverse (1838-1839)

Designer: Christian Gobrecht. Size: 30 mm. Weight: 13.36 g.
Composition: 90 percent silver (.3867 oz.), 10 percent copper.

In 1838, the representation of the denomination of the half dollar was changed from "50 Cents" to "Half Dol."

In that year, the first branch-mint coinage of half dollars began with the striking of 20 proofs at the newly established mint in New Orleans. Less than two dozen examples of this great rarity are known to exist today.

SEATED LIBERTY (1839-1891)

No motto above eagle
(1839-1853)

Designer: Christian Gobrecht. Size: 30.60 mm. Weight: 13.36 g. Composition: 90 percent silver (.3867 oz.), 10 percent copper. Note: One variety of the 1840 strike has smaller lettering; another used the old reverse of 1838. Varieties of 1842 and 1846 are distinguished by the size of the numerals in the date.

The Seated Liberty design made its appearance on the half dollar in 1839. The design was modified in the same year to include an extra fold of drapery from Liberty's left elbow. Christian Gobrecht is credited with the design, which was based on a Thomas Sully drawing.

In 1842, the lettering and date were increased in size to create small- and large-date varieties. The 1842-O small date is a rarity.

The most celebrated rarity of this type is the 1853-O with arrows and rays. Only a few exist.

Arrows at date, reverse rays
(1853)

Designer: Christian Gobrecht. Size: 30.60 mm. Weight: 12.44 g.
Composition: 90 percent silver (.36 oz.), 10 percent copper.

In an attempt to stop the disappearance of silver coins from circulation, the Act of Feb. 21, 1853, reduced the weight of the half dollar from 13.36 grams to 12.44 grams.

As with the other denominations, arrows were added at the date to denote the reduction in weight. In the case of the quarter and half dollar, a glory of rays, emanating from behind the eagle, was also added to the design.

Minted in Philadelphia and New Orleans, the "arrows and rays" half dollar is a popular one-year type coin.

Reverse rays removed
(1854-1855)

Designer: Christian Gobrecht. Size: 30.60 mm. Weight: 12.44 g.
Composition: 90 percent silver (.36 oz.), 10 percent copper.

James Ross Snowden, who had just entered into service as Mint director, is believed to have ordered the removal of the rays in 1854 from the reverse of the quarter and half dollar. The removal may have been meant to save expense on die sinking and die life.

This two-year type was struck at Philadelphia, New Orleans and, in 1855, at San Francisco. Mintage at San Francisco was a low 129,950, making the 1855-S a rare date.

Arrows at date removed
(1856-1866)

Designer: Christian Gobrecht. Size: 30.60 mm. Weight: 12.44 g. Composition: 90 percent silver (.36 oz.), 10 percent copper.

Although the weight would remain the same as the half dollars issued from 1853 through 1855, the arrows that had been placed next to the date in 1853 were removed in 1856. This same design was in use at the beginning of the Civil War and includes coins struck under the Confederate States of America.

More than 1.2 million half dollars were struck at the branch mint in New Orleans in early 1861 after Louisiana had officially seceded from the Union and just short of 1 million additional pieces were struck after the state joined the Confederacy.

The 1866-S "no motto" strike is scarce in all grades and had a mintage of just 60,000.

Motto above eagle
(1866-1873)

Designer: Christian Gobrecht. Size: 30.60 mm. Weight: 12.44 g. Composition: 90 percent silver (.36 oz.), 10 percent copper.

Largely through the urging of Pennsylvania minister M.R. Watkinson, the motto "In God We Trust" was adopted for use on the quarter, half dollar, gold $5, gold $10 and gold $20 in 1866. It had first appeared on the 2-cent piece in 1864.

The 1870-CC half dollar is scarce in all grades, with a mintage of 54,617.

Although Mint records indicate that some 5,000 1873-dated coins were struck at the San Francisco Mint prior to an increase in weight, brought on by the passage in February of that year of the Coinage Act of 1873, no specimens are known to exist and were likely melted.

Arrows at date
(1873-1874)

Designer: Christian Gobrecht. Size: 30.60 mm. Weight: 12.50 g. Composition: 90 percent silver (.3618 oz.), 10 percent copper.

Metric conversion was the reason for the increase in weight of the half dollar in 1873 as it had been for the dime and quarter. The half dollar's weight was raised from 12.44 grams to 12.50 grams. Arrows were added at the date to denote the weight increase.

A popular two-year type, the "with arrows" Seated Liberty half dollar was coined at Philadelphia, San Francisco and Carson City. The lowest mintage, 59,000, was recorded at the Carson City Mint in 1874.

Arrows at date removed
(1875-1891)

Designer: Christian Gobrecht. Size: 30.60 mm. Weight: 12.50 g. Composition: 90 percent silver (.3618 oz.), 10 percent copper.

Arrows, which had been placed next to the date in 1873 and 1874 to denote a weight increase, were removed in 1875. The weight stayed at the 12.5-gram level adopted in 1873. This design would be carried through the remainder of the Seated Liberty half dollars.

Mintages of the Seated Liberty half dollar were high from 1875 into 1878, when passage of the Bland-Allison Act forced the nation's mints to turn their attention to the production of the Morgan silver dollar. 1878 would also be the last year of branch-mint coinage of the Seated Liberty half dollar. Just 62,000 were struck at Carson City and 12,000 were minted in San Francisco. The latter is especially scarce in all grades.

Mintage at the mint in Philadelphia would continue through 1891, but at significantly lower levels after 1878. Mintage of the half dollar at Philadelphia, which stood at 1.378 million in 1878, plummeted to 5,900 the following year. Through 1890, coinage totals were very low and all dates are scarce in all grades. During its last year of coinage, the mintage rebounded to 200,600.

BARBER (1892-1915)

Designer: Charles E. Barber. Size: 30.60 mm. Weight: 12.50 g.
Composition: 90 percent silver (.3618 oz.), 10 percent copper.

Barber half dollars were struck at four mints, including Philadelphia, New Orleans, San Francisco and, beginning in 1906, at the newly established Denver branch. Key dates are the 1892-O, 1892-S and the 1897-S.

WALKING LIBERTY (1916-1947)

*Designer: Adolph A. Weinman. Size: 30.60 mm. Weight: 12.50 g.
Composition: 90 percent silver (.3618 oz.), 10 percent copper.*

One of the most popular 20th century designs, the Walking Liberty half dollar design was the work of Adolph A. Weinman. Weinman's Walking Liberty would be resurrected in 1986 for the silver American Eagle program.

From 1916 into the following year, the mintmark was shown on the obverse. In 1917, it was moved to the reverse, where it was displayed for the remainder of the Walking Liberty half dollar's coinage.

The 1917-D and 1917-S strikes come in obverse and reverse mintmark varieties. Those with the obverse mintmark are scarcer.

Striking was constantly a problem with the Walking Liberty half dollar. Several dates are found weakly struck, particularly noticeable on Liberty's left hand as it crosses the body and on the head and breast detail of Liberty.

The 1941-S is a leader among notable weakly struck dates in this series. Dates in strong demand, even in the lowest grades, include the 1921, 1921-D, and the 1938-D.

FRANKLIN (1948-1963)

Designer: John R. Sinnock. Size: 30.60. Weight: 12.50 g.
Composition: 90 percent silver (.3618 oz.), 10 percent copper.

Statesman, philosopher and inventor Benjamin Franklin, long a popular subject of medallic art, made his first appearance on a regular-issue U.S. coin in 1948 with the introduction of the Franklin half dollar.

The 1949-S is generally considered the key date in this series, although striking problems with the bell lines on the reverse have proven other dates to be much rarer in fully struck condition. Notable in this regard are the San Francisco strikes of 1951 through 1954 and coinage of the 1960s.

KENNEDY (1964 TO DATE)

90 percent silver composition
(1964)

Designer: Gilroy Roberts and Frank Gasparro. Size: 30.60 mm. Weight: 12.50 g. Composition: 90 percent silver (.3618 oz.), 10 percent copper.

Following the assassination of President John F. Kennedy, the Mint moved quickly to honor the nation's fallen leader. The Kennedy design by Mint Engraver Gilroy Roberts replaced the Franklin design beginning in 1964. The heraldic eagle on the reverse is credited to Frank Gasparro.

Kennedy's popularity made the 1964 date plentiful even in uncirculated, as many of this high-mintage date were saved.

Coinage of the 90 percent silver 1964-dated Kennedy half dollars continued into 1965, with a total mintage in excess of 277.254 struck at the Philadelphia Mint and an additional 156.205 million coined in Denver. These figures were much higher than any previous coinage of half dollars.

40 percent silver composition
(1965-1970)

Designer: Gilroy Roberts and Frank Gasparro. Size: 30.60 mm. Weight: 11.50 g. Composition: clad layers of 80 percent silver and 20 percent copper bonded to a core of 79.10 percent copper and 20.90 percent silver (.148 total oz. of silver).

Rising costs of silver and the constant disappearance of the coins from circulation led the Mint to abandon the use of silver in all circulation coins in 1965, with the exception of the half dollar, which continued to be coined in a silver-clad composition. The new composition consisted of an outer shell of 80 percent silver and an inner core of .209 percent silver and .791 percent copper.

The 1970-D silver clad half dollar was available as part of Mint-marketed mint sets and was not released into circulation. The 1965 through 1969 issues containing 40 percent silver can still sometimes be found in circulation.

Clad composition
(1971-1974)

Designer: Gilroy Roberts and Frank Gasparro. Size: 30.60 mm. Weight: 11.34 g. Composition: clad layers of 75 percent copper and 25 percent nickel bounded to a pure copper core.

In 1971, the Mint abandoned use of silver in the half dollar and switched to the base-metal clad composition already in use in the dime, quarter and newly released Eisenhower dollar coin.

Bicentennial design, clad composition (1975-1976)

Designer: Gilroy Roberts and Seth Huntington. Size: 30.60 mm. Weight: 11.34 g. Composition: clad layers of 75 percent copper and 25 percent nickel bounded to a pure copper core.

A design competition held in honor of the U.S. Bicentennial and open to artists throughout the country led to new reverses for the quarter, half dollar and dollar coins struck in 1975 and 1976. The coins uniformly read "1776-1976" to celebrate the Bicentennial. Chosen for the half dollar was a design of Independence Hall by Seth Huntington.

Regular design resumed, clad composition (1977 to date)

Designer: Gilroy Roberts and Frank Gasparro. Size: 30.60 mm. Weight: 11.34 g. Composition: clad layers of 75 percent copper and 25 percent nickel bounded to a pure copper core.

Frank Gasparro's heraldic-eagle reverse returned to the Kennedy half dollar in 1977. Although largely an unused coinage denomination in today's commerce, suggestions to drop the half dollar from the roster of circulation U.S. coins have yet to come to fruition.

DOLLARS

FLOWING HAIR (1794-1795)

Designer: Robert Scot. Size: 39-40 mm. Weight: 26.96 g.
Composition: 89.24 percent silver (.7737 oz.), 10.76 percent copper.

The nation's first silver dollar was designed by Robert Scot and featured a flowing hair Liberty facing right on the obverse. A small eagle perched on a cloud within a wreath appeared on the reverse.

Mintage of the first-year (1794) issue was a low 1,758, with only around 100 thought to remain in existence.

Most collectors who want an example of Scot's Flowing Hair dollar will opt for the 1795 issue, with a higher mintage of 160,295. It is, however, also scarce.

DRAPED BUST (1795-1803)

Small eagle
(1795-1798)

Designer: Robert Scot. Size: 39-40 mm. Weight: 26.96 g.
Composition: 89.24 percent silver (.7737 oz.), 10.76 percent copper.

Modeled after a drawing by portrait artist Gilbert Stuart, the Draped Bust design by Robert Scot was introduced on the dollar in 1795. The reverse continued to portray a small eagle perched on a cloud and surrounded by the wreath. It was the same design that appeared on the prior Flowing Hair dollar in 1794 and 1795.

Coins struck during this period vary largely in the number and placement of stars. The stars were meant to represent the number of states in the Union.

Mintages of this type were low. The coin saw very little domestic use and was often exported.

Heraldic eagle
(1798-1803)

Designer: Robert Scot. Size: 39-40 mm. Weight: 26.96 g.
Composition: 89.24 percent silver (.7737 oz.), 10.76 percent copper.

Silver dollars continued to be minted in between 1798 and 1803, though the coins did not circulate and were constantly exported.

The Draped Bust heraldic eagle design appeared on arguably the most famous of all U.S. coins, the 1804 silver dollar. The coin is termed by collectors "the king of American coins." Although Mint records indicate that 19,570 1804 silver dollars were struck, research by Eric P. Newman and Kenneth E. Bressett has shown that all of the 15 known specimens were struck much later. The first eight, for example, were minted in 1834 for inclusion in presentation cases to be given to foreign dignitaries.

Restrikes were then made in the late 1850s, including one now part of the collection at the Smithsonian Institution, which was struck over a Swiss shooting taler.

Rare proof restrikes of the 1801-1803 dates are also known, which were struck during the late 1850s at the U.S. Mint in Philadelphia.

GOBRECHT (1836-1839)

Designer: Christian Gobrecht. Size: 38.1 mm. Weight: 26.73 g.
Composition: 90 percent silver (.7736 oz.), 10 percent copper.

The failure of early examples of the silver dollar to enter or remain in circulation led President Thomas Jefferson to order a halt to its coinage. It did not resume until 1836 when Christian Gobrecht, a former bank note engraver, prepared dies based on drawings of a seated Liberty by Thomas Sully and a flying eagle by Titian Peale.

The placement of Gobrecht's name on the obverse die brought criticism and it had to be moved to the base. These first pieces and those dated 1838 are generally considered to have been struck for circulation.

Unlike the plain-edge 1836 circulation Gobrecht dollars, the 1839 circulation strikes had a reeded edge with 13 stars around the obverse design and were without stars on the reverse.

Restrikes of the 1836, 1838, and 1839 Gobrecht dollar were made during the late 1850s. In many cases, they are rarer than the originals.

SEATED LIBERTY (1840-1873)

No motto
(1840-1866)

Designer: Christian Gobrecht. Size: 38.10 mm. Weight: 26.73 g. Composition: 90 percent silver (.7736 ounce), 10 percent copper.

In 1840, full-scale production of the silver dollar began again in earnest. Featured was a modeling of Christian Gobrecht's Seated Liberty for the obverse. A heraldic eagle, similar to that already in use on the half dollar and quarter dollar, appeared on the reverse.

In the face of burgeoning gold supplies from California, silver prices shot up. Any chance that silver dollars would circulate was subsequently hindered. Unlike the half dimes, quarters and half dollars, which had been reduced in weight to a subsidiary level, the silver dollar's weight had not been changed, largely because it represented the unit of value.

The first branch-mint coinage of silver dollars came in 1846 when the New Orleans Mint struck 59,000 Seated Liberty dollars. Rarities include the 1851 and 1852 Philadelphia strikes, with mintages of 1,300 and 1,100, respectively. Restrikes of both of these dates are known in proof.

No dollars were struck for circulation in 1858 and only a small number of proofs were issued.

Motto added on reverse
(1866-1873)

Designer: Christian Gobrecht. Size: 38.10 mm. Weight: 26.73 g.
Composition: 90 percent silver (.7736 ounce), 10 percent copper.

In 1866, the addition of the religious motto "In God We Trust" created an additional variety of the Seated Liberty dollar.

This type includes several rare dates. Chief among these is the 1870-S. Fewer than one dozen specimens of an unknown original mintage have surfaced.

Although it is believed that 700 dollars were struck at the San Francisco Mint bearing an 1873 date, no specimens are known to exist.

Also rare are the Carson City dollars of 1871 through 1873, with mintages of 1,376, 3,150 and 2,300, respectively.

TRADE (1873-1885)

Designer: William Barber. Size: 38.1 mm. Weight: 27.22 g.
Composition: 90 percent silver (.7878 oz.), 10 percent copper.

The Trade dollar was one of those brilliant ideas that never quite panned out. Proposed as a means to compete with the Spanish and Mexican silver coins in the Orient market, the heavy, 420-grain U.S. Trade dollar never found its market.

Made legal tender in the United States for payments up to $5, the Trade dollar soon became a nuisance in this country. The unwanted coins, which found little of the hoped acceptance in the Orient, flooded back into the United States. They were also produced by depositors for domestic circulation.

By 1876, the value of the Trade dollar had fallen to a significant discount below its face value. Under pressure, Congress demonetized the coin in 1876, while allowing its continued mintage for export. Although production for circulation ended in 1878, proofs continued to be struck in very limited numbers through 1885.

By the 1880s, many of the unwanted, discounted coins had gravitated eastward. The Trade dollars were often paid out to unsuspecting workers at full face value. In 1887, by which time many of the Trade dollars had fallen into the hands of speculators, the government began redeeming coins that were not mutilated. Some 7,689,056 pieces were gathered and melted. Those pieces that saw circulation in the Far East can be recognized by chop marks added by merchants who accepted the coins.

Among regular-issue dates, the 1878-CC is a rarity. Although 97,000 were struck, more than 44,000 are known to have been melted by the Mint. The proof-only issues of 1879 through 1885 are also rare. The 1884, with a mintage of 10, and the 1885, with a mintage of five, are great rarities.

MORGAN (1878-1921)

Designer: George T. Morgan. Size: 38.10 mm. Weight: 26.73 g.
Composition: 90 percent silver (.7736 oz.), 10 percent copper.

A limited victory was achieved for the forces of free silver with the passage of the Bland-Allison Act of 1878. Free-silver advocates claimed the elimination of the silver dollar had been surreptitiously obtained during congressional passage of the Coinage Act of 1873. They tagged it as the "Crime of 1873," and ridiculously blamed it for the hardships and economic depression following the Civil War. The free silver advocates gained popular and political support. In the presidential election of 1896, the cause's greatest champion, William Jennings Bryan, was defeated.

The Bland-Allison Act required the Treasury to purchase between $2 million to $4 million in silver ore from domestic producers each month to be turned into silver dollars. Today, because of the vast production of silver dollars, many dates in the Morgan dollar series are plentiful. However, subsequent meltings, including nearly 270 million melted as a result of the Pittman Act of 1918, helped to create a number of rarities.

Among the rarest are the 1889-CC, the 1893-S and the 1894. Of a listed mintage of 12,880 1895 Morgan dollars, only a limited number of proofs are known to exist.

No silver dollars were minted from 1905 through 1920. Coinage of the Morgan dollar resumed in 1921, but the design was replaced in that same year by one marking the restoration of world peace.

PEACE (1921-1935)

High relief (1921)

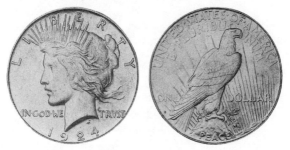

Designer: Anthony De Francisci. Size: 38.10 mm. Weight: 26.73 g.
Composition: 90 percent silver (.7736 oz.), 10 percent copper.

World War I was the "war to end all wars" and the Peace dollar was to be the coin to honor the lasting peace. Designed by Anthony De Francisci and modeled after his wife Teresa, the first-year's issue was struck in high relief. This proved to be impractical for large-scale production, but provided a popular variety for collectors.

Regular relief (1922-1935)

Designer: Anthony De Francisci. Size: 38.10 mm. Weight: 26.73 g. Composition: 90 percent silver (.7736 oz.), 10 percent copper.

Beginning in 1922, the Peace dollar was struck in a lower relief. The 1928 is considered the key date and has the series' lowest mintage, at 360,649.

EISENHOWER (1971-1978)

Eagle reverse
(1971-1974)

Designer: Frank Gasparro. Size: 38.10 mm. Weight: 22.68 g. Composition: clad layers of 75 percent copper and 25 percent nickel bounded to a pure copper core.

Although generally referred to as a "silver dollar," the Eisenhower dollar was the first U.S. dollar to be struck for circulation in base metal. With the exception of special 40 percent silver issues struck solely for collectors, the entire issue was a clad composition of copper and nickel. Designed by Mint Chief Engraver Frank Gasparro, the coin's obverse honored former President Dwight D. Eisenhower, while the reverse commemorated the first landing on the moon.

Bicentennial design
(1975-1976)

Designer: Frank Gasparro and Dennis R. Williams. Size: 38.10 mm.
Weight: 22.68 g. Composition: clad layers of 75 percent copper and 25 percent nickel
bounded to a pure copper core.

The reverse of the Bicentennial version of the Eisenhower dollar shows the Liberty Bell superimposed over the moon. It was designed by Dennis R. Williams, who was one of the winners of a design competition that saw new reverses introduced on the quarter dollar, half dollar and dollar to mark the nation's 200th birthday. Struck in 1975 and 1976, it used the dual date of "1776-1976."

Regular design resumed
(1977-1978)

Designer: Frank Gasparro. Size: 38.10 mm. Weight: 22.68 g. Composition: clad layers of 75 percent copper and 25 percent nickel bounded to a pure copper core.

In 1977, coinage of the Eisenhower dollar continued with Frank Gasparro's original reverse of an eagle landing on the moon replacing the Bicentennial design minted in 1975 and 1976.

ANTHONY (1979-1999)

Designer: Frank Gasparro. Diameter: 26.50 mm. Weight: 8.10 g. Composition: clad layers of 75 percent copper and 25 percent nickel bonded to a pure copper core.

In 1979, faced with the continuing problem of the short life span and high production cost of paper money, the Mint introduced a new mini-dollar. It hoped the coin would gain acceptance in circulation and supplant the paper dollar.

The new dollar coin featured suffragette Susan B. Anthony and a reduced adaptation of the Eisenhower dollar reverse. It measured 26.5 millimeters, as compared to the former clad dollar of 38.1 millimeters. The new dollar's similarity in size to the quarter led to a general unpopularity with the public.

Coinage of the original Anthony dollar was from 1979 through 1981. Coinage of the Anthony dollar resumed in 1999 for one year and was then supplanted by the Sacagawea golden dollar.

SACAGAWEA (2000-2008)

Designer: Glenna Goodacre, Thomas D. Rogers Sr. Diameter: 26.50 mm. Weight: 8.07 g.
Composition: .770 copper, .120 zinc, .070 manganese outer layer bonded to pure copper core.
Note: A variety of the 2000-P Sacagawea dollar struck from pattern hubs was released with
the wing and tail feathers on the coin's reverse more pronounced than on the regular strikes.
These were found in boxes of Cheerios cereal. The variety wasn't discovered until 2005, and
not all of the coins placed in the boxes were those of the pattern design.

The golden mini-dollar was introduced in 2000 with an obverse design by Glenna Goodacre. Goodacre won a national competition for the government's next attempt to circulate a small base-metal dollar coin. Goodacre's representation was of Sacagawea, the Native American Shoshone guide to the Lewis and Clark Expedition. Sacagawea carries her infant son, John Baptiste.

The reverse had an eagle in flight by Mint Engraver Thomas D. Rogers Sr.

NATIVE AMERICAN (2009 TO DATE)

Diameter: 26.50 mm. Weight: 8.07 g. Composition: .770 copper, .120 zinc, .070 manganese outer layer bonded to pure copper core. Note: Edge lettering on these coins shows the date, mintmark and "E Pluribus Unum." Edge lettering varieties exist, including examples in which the lettering was left off entirely.

In 2009, the U.S. Mint began issuing the Native American dollar series. The program was halted recently, except for the production of collector coins. The obverse design carries the Glenna Goodacre depiction of Sacagawea found on the Sacagawea dollar. The reverse designs celebrate "the important contributions made by Indian tribes and individual Native Americans to the history and development of the United States."

PRESIDENTIAL (2007-2016)

Diameter: 26.50 mm. Weight: 8.07 g. Composition: .770 copper, .120 zinc, .070 manganese outer layer bonded to pure copper core. Note: The 2007-2008 Presidential dollars had the legends "E Pluribus Unum," "In God We Trust" and the date and mintmark on the coin's edge. In 2009, the motto "In God We Trust" was moved to the coin's obverse. Edge lettering varieties exist, including examples in which the lettering was left off entirely.

In 2007, the U.S. Mint began issuing the Presidential dollar series. These coins are only permitted to show former presidents who have been deceased for more than two years. The series was slated to run into 2016, but recently the Mint halted production for circulation. The coins will continue to be produced for collectors. Each of the coins has a common reverse design depicting the Statue of Liberty. The coins also included edge incused inscriptions. The schedule is for four coins a year as follows:

2007

George Washington (1789-1797); John Adams (1797-1801); Thomas Jefferson (1801-1809); James Madison (1809-1817).

2008

James Monroe (1817-1825); John Quincy Adams (1825-1829); Andrew Jackson (1829-1837); Martin Van Buren (1837-1841).

2009

William Henry Harrison (1841); John Tyler (1841-1845); James K. Polk (1845-1849); Zachary Taylor (1849-1850).

2010

Millard Fillmore (1850-1853); Franklin Pierce (1853-1857); James Buchanan (1857-1861); Abraham Lincoln (1861-1865).

2011

Andrew Johnson (1865-1869); Ulysses S. Grant (1869-1877); Rutherford B. Hayes (1877-1881); James Garfield (1881).

2012

Chester A. Arthur (1881-1885); Grover Cleveland (1885-1889); Benjamin Harrison (1889-1893); Grover Cleveland (1893-1897).

2013

William McKinley (1897-1901); Theodore Roosevelt (1901-1909); William Howard Taft (1909-1913); Woodrow Wilson (1913-1921).

2014

Warren Harding (1921-1923); Calvin Coolidge (1923-1929); Herbert Hoover (1929-1933); Franklin D. Roosevelt (1933-1945)

2015

Harry S. Truman (1945-1953); Dwight D. Eisenhower (1953-1961); John F. Kennedy (1961-1963); Lyndon B. Johnson (1963-1969).

2016

Richard M. Nixon (1969-1974); Gerald Ford (1974-1977); Ronald Reagan (1981-1989).

GOLD
DOLLARS

LIBERTY HEAD, TYPE 1
(1849-1854)

Designer: James B. Longacre. Size: 13 mm. Weight: 1.672 g.
Composition: 90 percent gold (.0484 oz.), 10 percent copper.

The expression of the basic unit of value in gold did not come until 1849, after the discovery of gold in California. The first gold dollars measured 13 millimeters in diameter. The small size caused a number of problems, including confusion with silver coins of roughly the same size. Additionally, the small size made the coins easy to lose. These Type 1 gold dollars were struck from 1849 through 1854 at the Philadelphia, Charlotte, Dahlonega, San Francisco and New Orleans mints.

The 1849 coinage is known in open- and closed-wreath varieties. The 1849-C "open wreath" is a great rarity, with only a handful remaining.

All dates of this type are scarce and mintages were often extremely low, especially at the branch mints. The 1854-D is a key date, with just 2,935 minted.

SMALL INDIAN HEAD, TYPE 2
(1854-1856)

Designer: James B. Longacre. Size: 15 mm. Weight: 1.672 g.
Composition: 90 percent gold (.0484 oz.), 10 percent copper.

In 1854, the Type 1 Liberty Head gold dollar was replaced by a larger, thinner gold dollar, with the obverse modeled after the gold $3 piece. The reverse displayed a wreath of the type that would be used two years later on the Flying Eagle cent.

The Type 2 gold dollar was notorious for its poor striking qualities, noticeable especially at the centers.

The highest mintage of this type came in 1854 and 1855 at the Philadelphia Mint, with 783,943 and 758,269 struck, respectively. Still, all are scarce.

The rarest date is the 1855-D of which only 1,811 were minted. Very few remain in existence. In that same year, the New Orleans Mint struck its last gold dollar with a mintage of 55,000.

LARGE INDIAN HEAD, TYPE 3
(1856-1889)

Designer: James B. Longacre. Size: 15 mm. Weight: 1.672 g. Composition: 90 percent gold (.0484 oz.), 10 percent copper. Note: Two varieties of the 1856 strike are distinguished by whether the "5" in the date is slanted or upright. "Closed-3" and "open-3" varieties of the 1873 strike are known and are distinguished by the amount of space between the upper left and lower left serifs in the "3."

Striking problems with the Type 2 gold dollar led to yet another redesign in 1856. This included lowering the relief and widening the head.

Rarities include the 1856-D (1,460 struck), 1857-D (3,533), 1859-D (4,952), 1860-D (1,566), 1861-D (1,250), 1870-S (3,000) and the 1875 (420 struck).

The 1861-D was apparently struck after the Confederate States of America had taken over the Dahlonega Mint. Mintage is unknown.

GOLD
$2.50

CAPPED BUST RIGHT (1796-1807)

No stars
(1796)

Designer: Robert Scot. Size: 20 mm. Weight: 4.37 g.
Composition: 91.67 percent gold (.1289 oz.), 8.33 percent silver and copper.

Robert Scot is credited with the design of the nation's first gold $2.50 piece, or quarter eagle. It employed the same obverse as the half eagle introduced the year prior. The reverse of the quarter eagle showed a new heraldic eagle design, which would later become standard on U.S. gold and silver coins.

This rare one-year type, with a mintage of just 963 coins, lacked stars on the obverse, but did display 16 stars on the reverse. The stars represented the states in the Union. Tennessee, the 16th state, had been admitted in June of that year.

As with much of the gold series, melting contributed to the scarcity of often already low-mintage dates.

Stars
(1796-1807)

Designer: Robert Scot. Size: 20 mm. Weight: 4.37 g. Composition: 91.67 percent gold (.1289 oz.), 8.33 percent silver and copper. Note: Varieties of the 1804 strike came with 13 or 14 stars on the obverse.

Shortly after coinage of the gold $2.50 pieces began in 1796, the obverse design was changed to include 13 stars, representing the first 13 states. The number of stars on the reverse was dropped from an original count of 16.

Mintage of the gold $2.50 was sporadic and total output was low. Estimates of the number of 1796 "with stars" coins struck are placed at 432. The following year's mintage was lower, with 427 believed to have been coined.

The highest mintage of this Capped Bust gold $2.50 came in 1807, with 6,812 struck. No gold $2.50 pieces were minted after 1798 until 1802.

CAPPED BUST LEFT (1808)

Designer: John Reich. Size: 20 mm. Weight: 4.37 g. Composition: 91.67 percent gold (.1289 oz.), 8.33 percent silver and copper.

In 1808, John Reich's portrait of a capped Liberty facing left was placed on the gold $2.50 coin. It had been adopted the year prior for the gold $5 coin.

This rare one-year type had a mintage of just 2,710. Coinage of the gold $2.50 piece ended in 1808 and did not resume until 1821.

CAPPED HEAD LEFT (1821-1834)

Designer: Robert Scot. Size: 18.5 mm (1821-1827); 18.2 mm (1829-1834). Weight: 4.37 g.
Composition: 91.67 percent gold (.1289 oz.), 8.33 percent silver and copper.

By the time coinage of the gold $2.50 began again in 1821, its diameter had been slightly reduced and its design changed to one by Robert Scot.

Mintages were low, generally between the range of 2,000 to 6,000 per year. The bottom came in 1826 when only 760 gold $2.50 pieces were minted.

The introduction of a close collar during the minting process in 1829 further reduced the diameter of the pieces struck thereafter.

Due to melting, all dates of this design type are rare. A celebrated rarity is the 1834 date with the motto "E Pluribus Unum." The motto was dropped from the gold $2.50 in 1834, when the coin was redesigned. However, 4,000 gold $2.50 coins were struck of the old design before mintage began of the redesigned gold $2.50. Fewer than one dozen of the 1834 "with motto" gold $2.50 pieces are believed to exist.

CLASSIC HEAD (1834-1839)

Designer: William Kneass. Size: 18.2 mm. Weight: 4.18 g.
Composition: 89.92 percent gold (.1209 oz.), 10.08 percent silver and copper.

In 1834, the weights of the gold $2.50 and $5 pieces were lowered. The Liberty design was also remodeled by Mint engraver William Kneass. Gone was the liberty cap seen on prior issues. In its place was a ribbon, which bound the hair and carried the word "Liberty." Also gone was the motto "E Pluribus Unum."

Mintages of Classic Head gold quarter eagles were much higher than in prior years of gold $2.50 production. The first-year mintage of the Classic Head gold $2.50 coin was 112,234, well exceeding the combined mintage of all prior gold quarter eagles.

The highest mintage of this type came in 1836 when the Philadelphia Mint churned out 547,986 gold $2.50 pieces.

Branch-mint coinage of the gold $2.50 coin would begin in 1838 at the Charlotte Mint. Mintage of this rare date was 7,880. One year later, coinage began at Dahlonega and New Orleans.

CORONET HEAD (1840-1907)

Designer: Christian Gobrecht. Size: 18 mm. Weight: 4.18 g. Composition: 90 percent gold (.1209 oz.), 10 percent copper. Note: Varieties for 1843 are distinguished by the size of the numerals in the date. "Closed-3" and "open-3" varieties of the 1873 strike are known and are distinguished by the amount of space between the upper left and lower left serifs in the "3" in the date.

In 1840, Christian Gobrecht's Coronet design, which was already in use on the gold $10 coin, was placed on the gold $2.50. It would continue to be employed for the next 67 years.

There are several rare dates, including the famous proof-only 1841, of which one dozen are traced, and the 1854-S, with a miniscule mintage of 246 and with less than 10 specimens known to have survived.

In 1848, 1,389 gold $2.50 pieces were minted bearing a distinctive "Cal." marking above the eagle to show that these coins were struck from gold from California.

Also scarce are a number of the branch-mint issues and later date Philadelphia gold quarter eagles.

Among the rare dates are the 1854-S, of which just 243 were struck. Also notable are the low-mintage 1854-1856 Dahlonega gold $2.50 coins as well as the 1864, 1865, 1875, 1881 and 1885 Philadelphia strikes. The 1863 coinage was in proof only.

INDIAN HEAD (1909-1929)

Designer: Bela Lyon Pratt. Size: 18 mm. Weight: 4.18 g.
Composition: 90 percent gold (.1209 oz.), 10 percent copper.

The last design type for the gold quarter eagle was also the most unusual. Credited to Bela Lyon Pratt, from an idea by Dr. William Sturgis Bigelow, the new design featured an Indian on the obverse and an eagle on the reverse, both set (along with other design elements) sunken below the field.

However well-received artistically, the design brought criticism that the coins would not stack properly and that the many crevices readily attracted dirt and possibly transmitted diseases.

The 1911-D, with the design's lowest mintage (55,680), is the key date.

GOLD
$3

GOLD $3 (1854-1889)

*Designer: James B. Longacre. Size: 20.5 mm. Weight: 5.015 g.
Composition: 90 percent gold (.1452 oz.), 10 percent copper. Note: "Closed-3" and "open-3"
varieties of the 1873 strike are known and are distinguished by the amount of space
between the upper left and lower left serifs of the "3" in the date.*

Designed by James B. Longacre, the gold $3 series offers only scarce dates. Unfortunately, it has also been a popular target for counterfeiters, and caution must taken in purchasing these coins.

The series includes a classic rarity, the 1870-S, of which only one is known. A specimen was produced for placement in the cornerstone of the new San Francisco Mint. Whether the known specimen, formerly part of the Louis Eliasberg collection, is the example intended for the mint building's cornerstone or whether a second specimen resides inside the cornerstone is unknown.

Other rarities include the 1854-D, with a mintage of 1,120 and few survivors, and the 1875 and 1876 proof-only issues.

GOLD
$4

STELLA (1879-1880)

Flowing Hair
(1879-1880)

Designer: Charles E. Barber. Note: These are patterns, rather than coins struck for circulation. Examples in other metals also exist.

Popularity has earned these pattern coins a place in the regular series of U.S. coins. The gold $4, or "Stella" after the star on its reverse, was the brainchild of John A. Kasson, minister to Austria. It was argued that the gold $4 coin, which weighed 7 grams, would fit neatly into a metric system of coinage and would become an internationally accepted coin. Charles Barber is credited with the Flowing Hair design. The gold 1879 Flowing Hair, with a mintage of more than 400, is the most common. Less than two dozen of the gold 1880 date are known.

Coiled Hair
(1879-1880)

Designer: George T. Morgan. Note: These are patterns, rather than coins struck for circulation. Examples in other metals also exist.

George T. Morgan prepared what is known as the Coiled Hair version of the gold $4. Both dates of the gold Coiled Hair Stella are exceedingly rare.

GOLD
$5

CAPPED BUST RIGHT (1795-1807)

Small eagle
(1795-1798)

Designer: Robert Scot. Size: 25 mm. Weight: 8.75 g. Composition: 91.67 percent gold (.258 oz.), 8.33 percent silver and copper. Note: Two 1797 varieties are distinguished by the number of stars on the obverse.

The gold $5 piece or half eagle holds the distinction of being the first U.S. gold coin denomination minted, and the only denomination to have been struck at all of the U.S. mints except West Point.

Coinage of the gold $5 began in 1795 featuring a depiction of Liberty facing right on the obverse and a small eagle, perched on an olive branch with a wreath in its beak, on the reverse. The same basic design would appear on the gold $10 piece when coinage began in that same year. The obverse depiction of Liberty would also grace the gold $2.50 coin when it was introduced in 1796.

Mintages, as with much of the early gold series, were low and survival rates poor. Values are, therefore, very high.

The 1798 Capped Bust gold $5 with small-eagle reverse is a great rarity, with around seven specimens known to exist.

Heraldic eagle
(1795-1807)

Designer: Robert Scot. Size: 25 mm. Weight: 8.75 g. Composition: 91.67 percent gold (.258 oz.), 8.33 percent silver and copper. Note: 1804 varieties are distinguished by the size of the "8" in the date. 1806 varieties are distinguished by whether the top of the "6" has a serif.

In 1798, the gold $5 coin's reverse was changed to a heraldic-eagle design. However, pieces dated 1795 and 1797 with the heraldic-eagle reverse are known to exist. These are thought to have been made in 1798, possibly as emergency issues due to the yellow fever epidemics that led to several Mint shutdowns.

The 1795 and 1797 coinage with the heraldic-eagle reverse are great rarities. The 1797 date features 15 stars on the obverse as well as a piece showing 16 stars.

Many varieties are known and are distinguished by the size of the date punches and the number of stars on the reverse. The 1798, for example, was minted with a 13- or 14-star reverse.

Overdates are also prevalent. One of the more unusual is the 1802/1, which is of special interest because no gold $5 coins were minted bearing an 1801 date.

CAPPED DRAPED BUST LEFT
(1807-1812)

Designer: John Reich. Size: 25 mm. Weight: 8.75 g. Composition: 91.67 percent gold (.258 oz.), 8.33 percent silver and copper. Note: 1810 varieties are distinguished by the size of the numerals in the date and the sized of the "5" in the "5D." on the reverse. 1811 varieties are distinguished by the size of the "5" in the "5D" on the reverse.

In 1807, John Reich's design of Liberty began appearing on the gold $5. The design was criticized at the time for displaying "the artist's fat mistress." As with the preceding design, numerous varieties and overdates exist. Rare examples of the 1808 coinage show an 8/7 overdate, and the entire mintage of 1809 was struck with a die showing a 9/8.

CAPPED HEAD
(1813-1834)

Designer: John Reich. Size: 25 mm. Weight: 8.75 g. Composition: 91.67 percent gold (.258 oz.), 8.33 percent silver and copper. Note: 1821 varieties are distinguished by whether the "2" in the date has a curved base or square base, and by the size of the letters in the reverse inscriptions. 1832 varieties are distinguished by whether the "2" in the date has a curved or square base and by the number of stars on the reverse. 1834 varieties are distinguished by whether the "4" has a serif at its far right.

Increases in world silver supplies during this period made gold the dearer metal. Gold coins disappeared from circulation soon after. Large portions of the original mintages of the Capped Head half eagle were melted, creating some highly prized, high-price rarities. High on the list are the 1815, with an original mintage of 635, of which only a dozen or so are known to exist, and the 1822, with an original mintage of 17,796 and only three known. Two of these specimens are in the Smithsonian Institution's collection.

Other rarities of this type include the 1819, the 1825/4, and the 1829 "large planchet."

The use of a close coinage collar, beginning in 1829, made the size of the half eagle somewhat smaller. The 1829 "small planchet" half eagle is a rarity, with around a dozen known. An interesting mistake created the 1832 "blundered die" variety, which shows only 12 obverse stars instead of the correct 13 stars.

CLASSIC HEAD (1834-1838)

Designer: William Kneass. Size: 22.5 mm. Weight: 8.36 g. Composition: 1834-1836 89.92 percent gold (.258 oz.), 10 percent silver and copper; 1837-1838 90 percent gold (.242 oz.), 10 percent copper. Note: 1834 varieties are distinguished by whether the "4" in the date has a serif at its far right.

Congress lowered the weight of all gold denominations in 1834 in an attempt to combat their constant melting. The weight of the gold $5 piece was dropped from 8.75 grams to 8.36 grams.

To readily distinguish the new lower weight gold $5 coins, the motto "E Pluribus Unum" was removed from above the eagle on the coin's reverse.

William Kneass redesigned Liberty, her liberty cap disappearing in the new design.

Mintages were much higher than previous issues, with 657,460 struck in the first year alone. The reduced weight also helped keep the coins in circulation and survival rates are much higher.

Branch-mint coinage of the gold $5 began in 1838 at the Charlotte (17,179 struck) and Dahlonega (20,583) facilities.

CORONET HEAD (1839-1908)

No motto
(1839-1866)

Designer: Christian Gobrecht. Size: 21.6 mm. Weight: 8.359 g. Composition: 90 percent gold (.242 oz.), 10 percent copper. Note: Varieties of the 1842 Philadelphia strikes are distinguished by the size of the letters in the reverse inscription. Varieties of the 1842-C and –D strikes are distinguished by the size of the numerals in the date. Varieties of the 1843-O strikes are distinguished by the size of the letters in the reverse inscriptions.

In 1839, following after the redesign of the gold eagle, the half eagle would bear Christian Gobrecht's Coronet Head.

This long-lived design continued in use through 1908. Coinage of the Coronet half eagle began at the New Orleans Mint in 1840 and in 1854 at San Francisco.

The 1854-S is a great rarity, with a mintage of just 268 and only three specimens known to exist, one of which is in the national coin collection at the Smithsonian Institution.

With motto
(1866-1908)

Note: 1873 "closed-3" and "open-3" varieties are known and are distinguished by the amount of space between the upper left and lower left serifs of the "3" in the date.

In 1866, the motto "In God We Trust" began appearing on silver denominations worth more than the dime and gold denominations worth $5 or more.

This type includes coinage from Carson City and Denver, rounding out the seven mints that would strike the gold $5. Survival rates on many of the early dates of this type were low. Rarities include the 1875, with just 220 minted for circulation, and the proof-only 1887 issue, of which only 87 were struck.

INDIAN HEAD (1908-1929)

Designer: Bela Lyon Pratt. Size: 21.6 mm. Weight: 8.359 g.
Composition: 90 percent gold (.242 oz.), 10 percent copper.

In 1908, Bela Lyon Pratt's Indian Head gold $5 was introduced, showing the design detail sunken below the field. The new design was part of a general redesign of the nation's coinage. Inspired by President Theodore Roosevelt, the new designs were meant to be more artistic.

Top rarities in the Indian Head gold $5 series include the 1909-O and 1929.

GOLD
$10

CAPPED BUST (1795-1804)

Small eagle
(1795-1797)

Designer: Robert Scot. Size: 33 mm. Weight: 17.5 g. Composition: 91.67 percent gold (.5159 oz.), 8.33 percent silver and copper.

Until the introduction of the gold $20 in 1850, the gold $10, or eagle, was the highest denomination U.S. gold coin struck. The first pieces, released in very limited mintages from 1795 through 1797, bore Robert Scot's Capped Bust design on the obverse and his small-eagle design on the reverse. The same design had begun appearing on the gold $5 the year prior.

All dates of this type are rare, even in low grades.

Heraldic eagle
(1797-1804)

Designer: Robert Scot. Size: 33 mm. Weight: 17.5 g. Composition: 91.67 percent gold (.5159 oz.), 8.33 percent silver and copper.

Robert Scot's heraldic-eagle reverse was placed on the gold $10 in 1797, having previously appeared on the gold $2.50 in 1796.

Constant melting of gold coins (which had become worth more on the bullion market than at face value) led to suspension of coinage of the eagle in 1804 after some 3,757 coins of that date had been minted.

In 1834, a classic rarity was created when, hoping to assemble diplomatic presentation cases of the nation's coinage, the Mint struck 1804-dated silver dollars and 1804-dated eagles. The dollar had not, however, been minted in 1804, coinage having been stopped with the 1803-dated dollar.

The gold $10 had been minted, but the new dies prepared for the 1834 coinage differed from those in use in 1804, including the addition of a beaded border and a different style of "4" in the date.

The 1804 "plain 4," as the 1834 coinage has come to be identified, is a famous rarity in the U.S. series, with only four specimens known to exist, all of which are in proof.

CORONET HEAD (1838-1907)

No motto
(1838-1866)

Designer: Christian Gobrecht. Size: 27 mm. Weight: 16.718 g. Composition: 90 percent gold (.4839 oz.), 10 percent copper.

Coinage of the gold $10 (first minted in 1795) ended in 1804 and did not resume until 1838. During the intervening period, most gold coinage was melted.

In 1834, Congress, reacting to the problems associated with the higher price of gold in the face of large supplies of silver, lowered the bullion weight of all gold coins in an attempt to keep the coins in circulation.

When coinage of the gold $10 resumed, in 1838, it was at the new lower weight of 16.718 grams as compared to the prior weight of 17.5 grams. Christian Gobrecht's Coronet design replaced the previous design by Robert Scot, and the coin's diameter dropped from 33 millimeters to 27 millimeters.

Branch-mint coinage of the gold $10 began in 1841 at the New Orleans Mint. The scarcest regular-issue date of this type is the 1858, with a mintage of 2,521.

Motto
(1866-1907)

Designer: Christian Gobrecht. Size: 27 mm. Weight: 16.718 g. Composition: 90 percent gold (.4839 oz.), 10 percent copper. Note: 1873 "closed-3" and "open-3" varieties are known and are distinguished by the amount of space between the upper and lower left serifs of the "3" in the date.

In 1866, the religious motto "In God We Trust" began appearing on the gold $10 coinage.

The 1875 is a great rarity. Less than 20 of the original mintage of 120 are thought to survive.

INDIAN HEAD (1907-1933)

No motto
(1907-1908)

Designer: Augustus Saint-Gaudens. Size: 27 mm. Weight: 16.718 g. Composition: 90 percent gold (.4839 oz.), 10 percent copper. Note: 1907 varieties are distinguished by whether the edge is rolled or wired, and whether the legend "E Pluribus Unum" has periods between each word.

The introduction of the Indian Head gold $10 was another one of the design changes inspired by President Theodore Roosevelt. An Indian headdress adorns Liberty, modeled by famed sculptor Augustus Saint-Gaudens after a bust originally prepared for the Victory statue in his Sherman Monument in New York. A standing eagle is shown on the coin's reverse.

The 1908 coinage is in both "no motto" and "motto" varieties—the motto, "In God We Trust," having been added in that year. The experimental pieces of 1907, featuring wire edge or rolled edge, are the great rarities.

Motto
(1908-1933)

Designer: Augustus Saint-Gaudens. Size: 27 mm. Weight: 16.718 g. Composition: 90 percent gold (.4839 oz.), 10 percent copper.

Protests over the release of so-called "godless" coins led to placement of the motto, "In God We Trust," on the gold $10 and the gold $20 in 1908. The motto had been left off of both denominations at President Theodore Roosevelt's request. Roosevelt is said to have considered the use of the Lord's name on a coin blasphemy.

Rarities include the 1920-S, 1930-S, and the 1933. The last of these is a classic rarity, for even though 312,500 1933-dated gold $10 eagles were struck, virtually the entire mintage was melted.

LIBERTY HEAD (1849-1907)

'Twenty D.,' no motto
(1849-1866)

Designer: James B. Longacre. Size: 34 mm. Weight: 33.436 g. Composition: 90 percent gold (.9677 oz.), 10 percent copper. Note: In 1861, the reverse was redesigned by Anthony C. Paquet, but it was withdrawn soon after its release. The letters in the inscription on the Paquet-reverse variety are taller than on the regular reverse.

In 1848, James Marshall discovered gold on Johann Augustus Sutter's property in Sacramento, Calif., and the California Gold Rush was on.

The desperate need for gold coins in the West and the influx of supplies of the precious metal led to the introduction of the gold $20, or double eagle, in 1850.

Represented by one known example is a pattern 1849-dated gold $20 in proof. It is currently housed in the national coin collection at the Smithsonian Institution in Washington, D.C.

Other rarities include the 1854-O (3,250 minted), the 1856-O (2,250), and the 1861 and 1861-S Paquet-reverse double eagles. Of the 1861-S Paquet-reverse gold $20 pieces, two or possibly three are thought to exist.

'Twenty D.,' with motto
(1866-1876)

Designer: James B. Longacre. Size: 34 mm. Weight: 33.436 g. Composition: 90 percent gold (.9677 oz.), 10 percent copper. Note: 1873 "closed-3" and "open-3" varieties are known and are distinguished by the amount of space between the upper left and lower left serif in the "3" in the date.

The motto, "In God We Trust," was added to the reverse design beginning in 1866.

The first-year issue of the Carson City Mint, the 1870-CC, is a great rarity, with a mintage of 3,789.

'Twenty dollars'
(1877-1907)

Designer: James B. Longacre. Size: 34 mm. Weight: 33.436 g.
Composition: 90 percent gold (.9677 oz.), 10 percent copper.

Mintages of this third type of Liberty double eagle were high and many dates are relatively common.

Still, there are some scarce, low-mintage dates including the 1879-O (2,325 struck), the 1881 (2,260), 1882 (630), 1885 (828), 1886 (1,106), 1891 (1,442), the 1891-CC (5,000) and the 1892 (4,523 struck).

In 1883, 1884 and 1887, the Philadelphia Mint struck only proofs.

SAINT-GAUDENS (1907-1933)

Roman numerals in date
No motto
(1907)

Designer: Augustus Saint-Gaudens. Size: 34 mm. Weight: 33.436 g. Composition: 90 percent gold (.9677 oz.), 10 percent copper. Notes: Lettered-edge varieties have "E Pluribus Unum" on the edge, with stars between the words.

In 1907, one of the most popular designs ever placed on a U.S. coin made its appearance on the double eagle. Designed by noted sculptor Augustus Saint-Gaudens, the obverse showed Liberty striding forward with a torch in her right hand and an olive branch in her left. The reverse displays a flying eagle.

The first specimens of 1907 struck for circulation were in high relief with the date in Roman numerals. Patterns of that year came in even higher relief, often termed extremely or ultra high relief. Specimens were struck with a plain (one known) or lettered edge and are famous rarities.

Arabic numerals in date
No motto
(1907-1908)

Designer: Augustus Saint-Gaudens. Size: 34 mm. Weight: 33.436 g.
Composition: 90 percent gold (.9677 oz.), 10 percent copper.

The high relief of the first Saint-Gaudens gold $20 double eagles, though visually stunning, was found to be impractical for regular coinage. Later issues, including 361,667 struck in 1907, were of lower relief and carried Arabic numerals.

In 2009, the U.S. Mint recreated the Saint-Gaudens ultra high relief $20 as a 1 ounce gold piece, with 115,178 specimens sold.

Motto
(1908-1933)

Designer: Augustus Saint-Gaudens. Size: 34 mm. Weight: 33.436 g.
Composition: 90 percent gold (.9677 oz.), 10 percent copper.

As with Augustus Saint-Gaudens' design for the gold $10, first examples of the gold $20 did not include the religious motto, "In God We Trust," as part of the design. Protests over the lack of the motto led to its placement on the coin's reverse beginning in 1908.

Rarities include the 1920-S, 1921 and 1927-D. Although 180,000 1927-D gold $20 pieces were struck, fewer than one dozen are now believed to exist. Also rare are the dates from 1929 through 1933.

In 1933, gold $20 coins were minted, but none were supposed to be placed in circulation. A limited number, however, did escape the Mint, and in the past, the Treasury has made a case for confiscating examples as being illegal to own. In 2002, a specimen sold for $7.59 million in a sale conducted in conjunction with the government. The Treasury has since confiscated an additional 10 specimens.

Glossary

Adjustment marks: Marks made by the use of a file to correct overweight planchets prior to striking. Adjusting the weight of planchets was a common practice at the first U.S. Mint in Philadelphia and was often carried out by women hired to weigh planchets and do any necessary filing.

Altered: A coin that has been changed after it left the Mint. Such changes are often to the date or mintmark of a common coin in an attempt to increase its value by passing it off to an unsuspecting buyer as rare.

Alloy: A metal or mixture of metals added to the primary metal in the coinage composition, often as a means of facilitating hardness during striking. For example, most U.S. silver coins contain an alloy of 10-percent copper.

Anneal: To soften with heat. In the minting process, planchets are annealed prior to striking.

Authentication: The act of determining whether a coin, medal, token or other related item is a genuine product of the issuing authority.

Bag marks: Scrapes and impairments to a coin's surface imparted following minting by contact with other coins. The term originates from the storage of coins in bags, but such marks can be incurred as coins leave the presses and enter hoppers. Larger coins are more susceptible to the marks, which have an effect on determining the grade and, therefore, the value of a given coin.

Base metal: A metal with low intrinsic value.

Beading: A form of design around the edge of a coin. Beading once served the purpose of deterring clipping or shaving parts of the metal by those looking to make a profit and then return the debased coin to circulation.

Blank: Often used in reference to the coinage planchet or disc of metal from which the actual coin is struck. Planchets or blanks are punched out of a sheet of metal by what is known as a blanking press.

Business strike: A coin produced for circulation.

Cast copy: A copy of a coin or medal made by use of a casting process in which molds are used to produce the finished product. Casting imparts a different surface texture to the finished product than striking does and often leaves traces of a seam where the molds came together.

Center dot: A raised dot at the center of a coin caused by the use of a compass to aid the engraver in the circular positioning of die devices, such as stars, letters and dates. Center dots are prevalent on early U.S. coinage.

Chop marks: A practice used by Oriental merchants as a means of guaranteeing the silver content of coins paid out. The merchants' chop marks, or stamped insignia, often obliterated the original design of the host coin. U.S. Trade dollars, struck for circulation from 1873-1878 and intended for use in trade with China, are sometimes found bearing multiple marks.

Clipping: The practice of shaving or cutting small pieces of metal from a coin in circulation. Clipping was prevalent in Colonial times as a means of surreptitiously extracting precious metal from a coin before placing it back into circulation. The introduction of beading and a raised border helped alleviate the problem.

Coin alignment: U.S. coins are normally struck with an alignment by which, when the coin is held by the top and bottom edge and rotated from side-to-side, the reverse will appear upside down.

Collar: A ring-shaped die between which the obverse and reverse coinage dies come together during striking. The collar is used to contain the outward flow during striking and can be used to produce edge reeding.

Commemorative: A coin issued to honor a special event or person. In the U.S., commemoratives are generally produced for sale to collectors and are not placed into circulation.

Copy: A replica of an original issue. Copies often vary in quality and metallic composition to the original. Since passage of the Hobby Protection Act (Public Law 93-167) of Nov. 29, 1973, it has been illegal to produce or import copies of coins or other numismatic items that are not clearly and permanently marked with the word "Copy."

Counterfeit: A coin or medal or other numismatic item made fraudulently, either for entry to circulation or for sale to collectors.

Denticles: The tooth-like pattern found around the border of a coin.

Die: A cylindrical piece of metal containing an incuse image that imparts a raised image when stamped into a planchet.

Die crack: A crack that develops in a coinage die after extensive usage, a defective die, or striking of harder metals. Die cracks, which often run through border lettering, appear as raised lines on the finished coin.

Device: The principal design element.

Double eagle: Name adopted by the Act of March 3, 1849, for the gold coin valued at 20 units or $20.

Eagle: Name adopted by the Coinage Act of 1792 for a gold coin valued at 10 units or $10.

Edge: The cylindrical surface of a coin between the two sides. The edge can be plain, reeded, ornamented or lettered.

Electrotype: A copy of a coin, medal or token made by electroplating.

Exergue: The lower segment of a coin, below the main design, generally separated by a line and often containing the date, designer's initials, and the mintmark.

Face value: The nominal legal-tender value assigned to a given coin by the governing authority.

Fasces: A Roman symbol of authority consisting of a bound bundle of rods and an ax.

Field: The flat area of a coin's obverse or reverse, devoid of devices or inscriptions.

Galvano: A reproduction of a proposed design from an artist's original model produced in plaster or another substance and then electroplated with metal. The galvano is then used in a reducing lathe to make a die or hub.

Glory: A heraldic term for stars, rays or other devices placed as if in the sky or as luminous.

Grading: The largely subjective art of providing a numerical or adjectival ranking of the condition of a given coin, token or medal. The grade is often a major determinant of the price of a given numismatic item.

Gresham's Law: Named for the 16th-century English financier Sir Thomas Gresham, an observation that when two coins with the same face value but with differing intrinsic value are in circulation at the same time, the one with the lesser intrinsic value will remain in circulation while the other is hoarded.

Half eagle: Name adopted by the Coinage Act of 1792 for a gold coin valued at five units or $5.

Hub: A piece of die steel showing the coinage devices in relief. The hub is used to produce a die that has the relief details incuse. The die is then used to produce the final coin, which looks similar to the hub. Hubs may be reused to make new dies.

Legend: The principal lettering of a coin, generally shown along the coin's outer parameter.

Lettered edge: Used to describe a coin or medal that has incuse or raised lettering on its edge.

Matte: A coin in which the surface of the coin has a granular or dull surface.

Magician's coin: The term sometimes used to describe a coin with two heads or two tails, made by alteration of a coin after it left the Mint.

Medal: Medals, often made to commemorate a person or an event, differ from coins in that they carry no recognized monetary value and, in general, are not produced with the intent to circulate as money.

Medal alignment: Medals are generally struck with the dies facing the same direction during striking. When held by the top and bottom edge and rotated from side-to-side a piece struck in this manner will show both the obverse and the reverse right side up.

Mintage: The total number of coins struck during a given time frame, generally one year.

Mintmark: A letter or other marking used on a coin's surface to identify the mint at which the coin originated.

Mule: The combination of two coinage dies not intended for use together.

Numismatics: The science, study or collecting of coins, tokens, medals, paper money and related items.

Obverse: The front or "heads" side of a coin, medal or token.

Overdate: Variety produced when one or more digits of the date are changed at the mint, generally to save on dies or to correct an error.

Overmintmark: Variety created at the Mint when a different mintmark is punched over an already existing mintmark, generally done to make a coinage die already punched for one mint serviceable at another.

Overstrike: A coin, token or medal produced using a planchet of a previously struck specimen.

Pattern: A proposed coinage design issued by the mint or authorized agent of a governing authority. Patterns can be in a variety of metals, thicknesses and sizes.

Phrygian cap: A close-fitting eggshell-shaped hat placed on the head of a freed slave when Rome was in its ascendancy. Hung from a pole, it was a popular symbol of freedom during the French Revolution and in 18th-century United States.

Planchet: A disc of metal or other material on which the image of the dies are impressed. Also sometimes called a blank.

Proof: A coin struck twice or more from specifically polished dies and polished planchets. Modern proofs are generally prepared with a mirror finish. Early 20th-century proofs were prepared with a matte surface.

Prooflike: A coin that exhibits some of the characteristics of a proof coin, but not all. Many Morgan dollars are found with prooflike surfaces, whereby the field will have a mirror background similar to that of a proof and design details are frosted as on some proofs.

Quarter eagle: Name adopted by the Coinage Act of 1792 for a gold coin valued at 2.5 units or $2.50.

Reeding: Serrated (tooth-like) ornamentation applied to the coin's edge during striking.

Relief: A design raised above the surface of a coin, medal or token.

Restrike: A coin, medal or token produced from original dies at a later date, often with the purpose of sale to collectors.

Reverse: The backside or "tails" side of a coin, medal or token, opposite from the principal figure of the design or obverse.

Rim: The raised area bordering the edge and surrounding the field.

Series: The complete group of coins of the same denomination and design and representing all issuing mints.

Token: A privately issued piece, generally in metal, with a represented value in trade or offer of service. Tokens are also produced for advertising purposes.

Type coin: A coin from a given series representing the basic design.

Variety: Any coin noticeably different in dies from another of the same design, date and mint.

Wire edge: Created when coinage metal flows between the coinage die and the collar, producing a thin flange of coin metal at the outside edge or edges of a coin.

ADJUSTMENT MARKS

During the operations of the first Philadelphia Mint, coin planchets judged to be too heavy were adjusted by strokes of a file prior to striking. To the chagrin of collectors, such adjustment marks were not obliterated by striking and are visible on many early U.S. coins.

ARROWS

Arrows were added to the date on the half dimes, dimes, quarters and half dollars of 1853 through 1855 to denote a reduction in weight. Arrows on the dimes, quarters and half dollars between 1873 and 1874 marked an increase in weight. The changes can be linked to the constantly fluctuating system of bimetallic coinage during the 19th century.

The discovery of gold in California in 1848 had an impact on the coinage system, and set Gresham's Law into effect. Plentiful supplies of gold drove the price of silver up and led to its disappearance from circulation. The Mint Act of 1853 reduced the weight of the half dime, dime, quarter and half dollar in proportional alignment with a 384-grain subsidiary dollar. Arrows were again added in 1873, but this time to signify a slight increase in the weight of the coins to a metric standard.

ARROWS AND OLIVE BRANCH

Rules of heraldry called for the warlike arrows shown on U.S. coins to be carried in the eagle's sinister (left) claw. When Robert Scot set about preparing the heraldic-eagle reverse found he apparently blundered the proper placement, putting the arrows in the eagle's right claw and the olive branch in the left. Or, perhaps the placement was an intentional act on the part of a young nation in a posturing of strength.

Scot's heraldic eagle reverse appears on half dimes (1800-1805), dimes (1798-1807), quarters (1804-1807), half dollars (1801-1807), silver dollars (1798-1803), quarter eagles (1796-1807), half eagles (1795-1807) and eagles (1795-1797).

BAG MARKS

The term "bag mark" refers to a nick or cut in the coin's surface that occurs after striking, but before the coin enters circulation. It comes directly from coin-to-coin contact, either in the hoppers at the mint, during bagging, or during transport and storage. Larger and heavier coins, such as the silver dollar, were more susceptible to bag marks. Much of the grading of an uncirculated coin is based on the number and severity of bag marks.

BUGS BUNNY QUARTER

Sometimes things get messed up in the minting process. Variety collectors are well aware of this and pursue such oddities. Shown here is a bit of an extra treat. There's a low value variety of the Franklin half dollar known as the Bugs Bunny variety due to what was likely the remnants of a die clash appearing at the mouth area of Benjamin Franklin. It's found most often on 1955 dates from the Philadelphia Mint. What makes this example more spectacular is that the half dollar dies with the minor damage were used on a planchet intended to produce a quarter dollar. This wrong planchet piece, with the added attraction of the Bugs Bunny variety, would find a welcome home in many collections.

CAST COPY

Casting leaves a much different look to the surface than coins, medals or tokens struck with pressure from a set of dies. Above is the surface of a fake Morgan dollar made by the use of casting molds. Compare it to the way metal flow lines look on the surface of a genuine coin (at right) struck using coinage dies and tons of pressure.

COIN VS. MEDAL ALIGNMENT

Coin alignment

When a U.S. coin is held by the edge between the thumb and forefinger and rotated on its axis from side-to-side, the reverse will be upside down. This is known as "coin alignment."

"Medal alignment" is normally used in striking medals, whereby the dies are both facing the same direction during striking. When a medal-aligned piece is turned from side-to-side, the reverse will be right side up.

The relationship of the dies is generally identified in written descriptions by employing two arrows. In the case of a coin struck with the more normal coin alignment, the first arrow is shown pointing upward and the second downward. In the case of medal alignment, both arrows point upward. The relationship becomes important in distinguishing certain 19th century restrikes. Some were struck from original dies but with medal alignment while the originals were struck with coin alignment.

Not all U.S. coins will display perfect coin alignment, but to have significant value to error collectors, such coins should be rotated at least 90 degrees from the normal position.

CUD

A cud is the term used by variety collectors to describe a major piece of the coinage die breaking away, and the impacted area on the subsequently minted coin. Cuds can be quite obvious, such as this Washington quarter on which only a portion of the "1" in the date remains visible, as the rest of the die has broken away.

DIE CLASHES

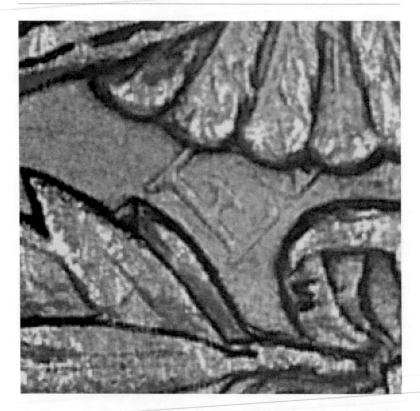

When the obverse and reverse dies come together during the minting process without a planchet in between, it can create some dramatic effects on the coins subsequently minted with the now-damaged dies. Die clashes often transfer the design from one die to the other. Look at this 1891-O Morgan dollar. In the area on the reverse between the eagle's tail feathers and the wreath, the "E" from "Liberty" from the coin's obverse design can be seen. There are many examples of clashed dies in other series as well, but this one is one of the more dramatic.

DIE CRACKS

Die cracking was a constant problem for the U.S. Mint during the 18th and 19th centuries. Once a crack developed in a die, metal would flow into the crack during the striking process, leaving a raised irregular line on the finished coin. Such cracks are often found running through legends and stars along a coin's perimeter. Die cracks are an interesting phenomenon of the minting process and useful to the numismatist in tracing the life of a coinage die, but generally have little to no effect on a coin's value.

DIE POLISHING

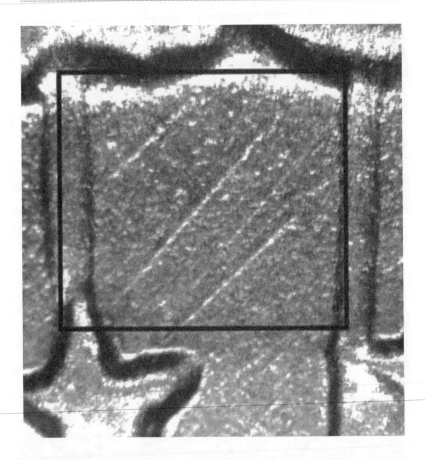

Sometimes coinage dies are polished at the mint, which can leave telltale signs on the minted coin's surface. Unlike scratches, which are incuse in the coin's surface, die polish lines (which are incuse on the coinage die) appear as raised lines on the coin's surface. These mint-caused polish lines will appear on other coins struck from the same dies.

DIME STRUCK BY CENT DIES

Some dramatic results can occur when a previously minted coin, in this case a Roosevelt dime, is struck by dies for another denomination. Note the denomination "Dime" from the reverse of a Roosevelt dime and the outline of Lincoln's shoulder from the obverse of a cent on this error coin.

FASCES

Much of the symbolism on modern coins can be traced to ancient times. The fasces, a bundle of rods bound to a battle-ax, was a symbol of authority during the Roman Empire. In the case of the Mercury dime, which shows the fasces entwined by an olive branch, Adolph Weinman, the artist, used the fasces to represent unity of strength; the battle-ax, the nation's willingness to defend itself; and the olive branch, the nation's love of peace.

MINTMARK

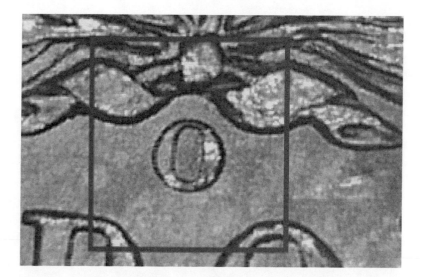

It's sometimes hard to believe that the addition, deletion, alteration, or appearance of an almost imperceptible mark on a coin could cause it to hold or lose substantial value. But that is exactly what can happen. Mintmarks, the minute letters found on either the obverse or reverse of most branch-mint coins, were first used on U.S. coins in 1838.

The opening of branch mints in Dahlonega, Charlotte and New Orleans presented the need to identify which mint produced a given coin. Later, the branch mints at San Francisco, Carson City, Denver and West Point would be represented by a mintmark. Philadelphia began putting its P mintmark on the war nickels of the 1940s and expanded its use in the 1980s.

Until the late 19th century, coin collectors focused on collecting coins of a given year, paying little or no attention to the mintmark. It wasn't until A.G. Heaton published "A Treatise on the Coinage of the United States Branch Mints" in 1893 that mintmarks became an important aspect of coin collecting and their value began to be appreciated and documented.

OVERMINTMARK

Since the first U.S. branch mints opened in the late 1830s, spurring the use of mintmarks, there have been many examples of what are known as "overmintmarks." Often done to save on coinage dies, a new mintmark is punched over the old mintmark. Examples are listed by numismatists with the mint of striking first, such as "D/S," in which case the coin was struck at Denver using a die originally intended for San Francisco. Often the under mintmark is readily visible.

STARS

In 1794, the question of how many stars to place on a U.S. coinage design was easily solved: Place 15 stars around the obverse design of the half dime, half dollar and silver dollar to represent the 15 states in the Union. This number included the new states of Vermont and Kentucky, which joined the Union in 1791 and 1792, respectively. But the admission of Tennessee as the 16th state in 1796 caused problems for the Mint and created varieties for collectors of early U.S. coinage.

In the half dollar series, for example, the admission of Tennessee led to the striking of both 15- and 16-star coins in 1796. By the following year the Mint had determined that continually adding stars to the nation's coinage for each new state was impractical. The solution was to show 13 stars representing the 13 original states. Again, new varieties were the result. The half dimes of 1797 were struck with 15, 16, or 13 stars; the dimes with 16 or 13 stars; half eagles with 15 or 16 stars; and the 1798 dollars with 15 or 13 stars.

The reuse of early coinage dies created some interesting combinations, including a 1799 dollar sporting 13 stars on the obverse and 15 stars on the reverse. By the beginning of the 19th century, 13 stars had become the accepted norm, with a few notable exceptions: an 1804 dime and quarter eagle with 13 and 14 stars, an 1817 large cent with 13 stars and 15 stars, the 1836 Gobrecht dollar, and the Kennedy half dollar with 50 stars around the reverse design and 13 stars within the glory emanating from the heraldic eagle.

1804 LARGE CENT

The most common test in determining genuine 1804 large cents from those bearing altered dates is the positioning of the numeral "0" in the date on the coin's obverse and the "O" in "Of" on the reverse. On a genuine 1804 large cent, those elements should be perfectly aligned. When a piece of paper is folded over the coin, the edge of the paper should run directly through the center of the numeral "0" and the letter "O" on the opposite side.

Don Taxay, in his *Counterfeit, Misstruck and Unofficial U.S. Coins,* provided an additional diagnostic. On the genuine 1804 large cent (at left), the second berry on the right extends below the right top vertical of the letter "E" in "One." Taxay noted that the 1804 cent bears a large 1/100th fraction found on only a few varieties of the 1803 cent. Such specimens, if altered to create an 1804 cent, would show the second berry in line with the right top vertical of the letter "E" in "One," rather than below it. Originals of the 1804 large cent were struck with a normal die or a broken die.

1817 LARGE CENT '15 STARS'

Was it simply a blunder that led to one of the most spectacular varieties of the Coronet large cents? No one seems to know for certain, but Robert Scot placed 15 stars around the border of the 1817 "15 stars" variety, rather than the standard 13 found on all other Matron Head cents through 1835. Although considered rare in uncirculated, this popular variety is available in lower grades.

1856 FLYING EAGLE CENT

The "5" in the date of the 1856 Flying Eagle cent can be used to distinguish genuine examples from those altered from an 1858 Flying Eagle. Genuine examples show a slanting "5," with the ball of the "5" extending behind the upright. The 1858 coins show the numeral "5" as vertical and the ball in line with the upright.

1858 FLYING EAGLE CENT

Two distinct varieties were struck of the 1858 Flying Eagle cent, large letters and small letters. The varieties are most easily identified by viewing the "AM" in the word "America" on the coin's obverse. On the large-letter variety, the legs of the "A" and "M" touch. On the small-letter variety, there is a noticeable gap between the letters.

1864 INDIAN HEAD CENT WITH 'L'

In 1864, the letter "L" representing the coin's designer, James B. Longacre, was added to the ribbon on the bronze Indian Head cent. As production of the 1864 "L" cents began late in the year, mintages were lower than for the 1864 cent without the "L." This accounts for the higher value of the 1864 "L" variety. A simple means of identifying even a heavily worn 1864 "L" cent is to note the tip of the Indian's bust. On the coins that carry the "L" the tip of the bust is pointed. On the specimens without the "L" the tip of the bust is rounded.

1877 INDIAN HEAD CENT

There are several keys to identifying a genuine 1877 circulation-strike Indian Head cent. The most common reference point is on the reverse. Like other Indian Head cents from the period, genuine specimens will generally exhibit a characteristic weakness at the bottom right angle of the "N" in "One" and on the "E" in "Cent." Also note that in the date, the second "7" extends below the first '7." Most counterfeits display the 7s in line.

1909 V.D.B. LINCOLN CENT

Shortly after its release into circulation, complaints began filtering into the Mint concerning the prominent placement of designer Victor D. Brenner's initials on the reverse of the Lincoln cent. In reality, the initials were less prominent than "Brenner," which appeared in the same position on the original models. No doubt use of the complete surname would have brought an even greater outcry, similar to what was heard when Christian Gobrecht's last name appeared above the date on the 1836 patterns of the Gobrecht dollar.

1909-S V.D.B. CENT

Shortly after the first Lincoln cents were released into circulation, the Mint altered the design by removing Victor D. Brenner's initials from the coin's reverse. The San Francisco strikes with the V.D.B. are highly sought after. Therefore, there are many outright fakes and alterations. A couple of points to watch for on the genuine specimens involve the "S" mintmark on the obverse and "B" from "V.D.B." on the reverse. The "S" mintmark's serifs should be vertical and parallel to each other. On the "B," the center crossbar will be diagonal, not horizontal.

ALTERED 1914-D LINCOLN CENT

The 1914-D Lincoln cent is a key in the Lincoln cent set and as such, is subject to counterfeiting and alteration. One of the most common ways to create a 1914-D from another coin is to take a 1944-D and alter the first "4," making it into a "1." One of the major problems with this, besides the visual remnants of the alteration on the coin's surface, is the unusually wide gap left between the "19" and the new "14" in the date (see the top photo). Also, the real 1914-D would not have Victor D. Brenner's initials, "V.D.B.," on the truncation of Lincoln's shoulder, where they appear on any Lincoln cent dated 1918 or later. (Lower left, V.D.B. on truncation; lower right real 1914-D)

1922 'NO D' LINCOLN CENT

Plugged and worn dies have generally been blamed as the culprits in the creation of the 1922 "no D" cent. The now-defunct American Numismatic Association Certification Service at one time identified three separate dies used in the production of the Denver cent without mintmarks. Examples can be found with portions of the "D" still visible. Also, wide differences in premiums exist and confusion reigns between a "plain" or "weak D" 1922 cent. Beware of counterfeits produced by the removal of the mintmark from 1922-D cents. (Both coins shown here are genuine.)

DOUBLED DIES 1955 AND 1972

Two of the most popular collectible doubled-die coins were struck at the Philadelphia Mint in 1955 and 1972. Both carry significant premiums in all grades and were created from obverse dies that doubled in the transfer from the working hub. Working dies were then produced by several blows from a positive die known as a hub. In the case of the 1955 and 1972 doubled dies, at least one of the strikes of the obverse working hub to an obverse working die was shifted out of alignment. All coins minted from the misstruck die presented an obviously doubled obverse and a normal reverse.

1955 'POORMAN'S DOUBLE DIE'

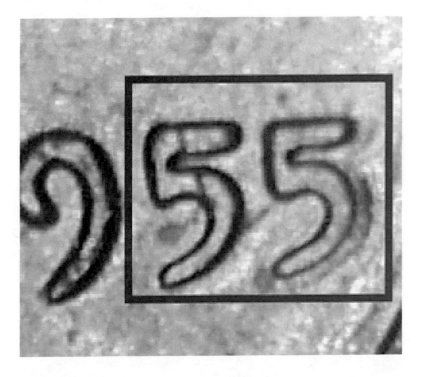

This relatively worthless variety gained notoriety after the release of the scarce doubled-die cent of 1955. The "Poorman's Double Die," as it was called, was promoted as a means of obtaining an inexpensive version of the popular 1955 doubled-die cent. The 1955 doubled die, which commands a hefty premium even in low grades, was created through an errant strike from a positive die, known as a hub, used to produce working dies. At least one of the blows from the hub was out of alignment, causing doubling in the working die. All coins struck from this die displayed this scarce form of prominent doubling. The "Poorman's Double Die," on the other hand, is nothing more than a die polishing variety and, therefore, of little more than curiosity value.

SMALL- AND LARGE-DATE 1960 CENTS

In 1960, a change in the master dies led to the creation of the small- and large-date Lincoln cents struck at the Philadelphia and Denver mints. The more valuable small-date cent variety can be distinguished from its large-date counterpart by the more compact appearance of the "6" and its shorter tail. Another diagnostic is the top of the "1" on the small-date cent, which aligns with the top of the "9." The large-date variety also shows the numerals as being slightly closer together.

ALTERED 1960 'SMALL DATE' CENT

As if to prove that no variety is safe from alteration, no matter how inexpensive or common, this 1960-D "small-date" Lincoln was converted into a slightly more valuable 1960 "small-date" by the removal of the "D" mintmark.

FAKE DOUBLE STRUCK IN COLLAR

Here's a 1964 Lincoln cent with a rotated image of Lincoln, the date, etc., as if the coin was struck by the coinage die a second time while it was still in the coinage collar. It is, however, a fake. A similar 1964-dated specimen recently sold on an online auction service as a real mint error. There are real errors in which the coin is double struck or more while in the coinage collar, but there are plenty of post-mint creations collectors need to be wary of when pursuing minting varieties.

LARGE- AND SMALL-DATE 1970-S CENTS

Large date

Small date

In 1970, a change in the master dies used to produce cents at the San Francisco Mint created the popular 1970-S small-date cent variety. The small-date cent can be most readily distinguished from its large-date counterpart by viewing the top part of the loop in the "9." On the large-date variety, this loop curves at a 45-degree angle toward the leg of the "9." On the more valuable small-date variety, this same loop turns more sharply in toward the body of the "9." The position of the "7" in the date can also be used to distinguish the varieties. On the large-date cent, the "7" appears to rest just below the remaining three digits in the date. On the small-date cent, the tops of all four digits are in line.

COUNTERFEIT 1972 DOUBLED-DIE CENT

This die-struck counterfeit 1972 doubled-die Lincoln cent was once purchased by a dealer as a genuine specimen. The tops of the doubled letters at left, particularly noticeable here on the counterfeit's "W" and "U" in "In God We Trust," don't extend as far up on the letter to the right as they do on a genuine specimen. Note, in comparison, the "U" on the genuine specimen. The tops of both vertical arms align with the top of the "U" to the right. On the counterfeit, the inside arm of the "U" is shorter. The left vertical arm of the "W" at left is also noticeably shorter than the left vertical arm of the "W" to its right.

LARGE- AND SMALL-DATE 1982 CENTS

Small date

Large date

The year 1982 was one of change for the Lincoln cent. The former brass composition was dropped in favor of copper-plated zinc. In that same year, modification of the coinage dies led to the creation of the so-called 1982 small-date cent. Circulation coinage at West Point, Denver and proofs struck in San Francisco used the old large-date dies. Philadelphia began coinage with the large-date dies before switching to the new small-date dies in September. It would strike both the brass and the copper-plated zinc composition cents with both the large-date dies and the small-date dies. The small-date die featured letters and a date with strongly beveled edges and a slightly lower relief to Lincoln's bust (see top image). The "8" in the date was also repositioned and appears more in line with the other numerals on the small-date variety. The upper loop of the "8" is also noticeably smaller than the lower loop.

SMALL- AND LARGE-MOTTO
1864 2-CENT PIECES

In 1864, the religious motto "In God We Trust" made its first appearance on the newly introduced 2-cent piece. Two varieties of the motto exist on the coins of 1864, large and small. The small-motto variety is the scarcer and more valuable of the two.

Several methods exist for easily identifying the small- and large-motto coins. On the small-motto variety the inside space in the letters "O" and "D" of "God" is wide and round. On the large-motto variety, it is narrow and oval. Another helpful reference point is the first "T" in the word "Trust." On the small-motto variety, the "T" touches the ribbon fold at its left (bottom image). It does not touch the ribbon fold on the large-motto variety. Also, on the small-motto coin, a stem can be seen on the leaf appearing below the word "Trust." The stem is absent from the large-motto variety.

1870-S SEATED HALF DIME

There was no record of the existence of an 1870-S half dime until 1978, when the only known specimen was found. Another example may exist in the cornerstone of the old San Francisco Mint, which was built in that year, but this is unverified. The exact location of the cornerstone, which this coin may have been intended for, is also unknown.

RACKETEER NICKEL

When the Liberty Head nickel was introduced in 1883, the first issues bore only the Roman numeral "V" on the coin's reverse to indicate its value. This, along with the nickel's similarity in size and weight to a gold half eagle, led to numerous pieces being gold plated and reeded so that the nickels could be passed as gold $5 pieces. These plated issues came to be known as Racketeer nickels. Later that same year, the problem was corrected by the addition of the word "Cents" below the wreath on the coin's reverse.

1913 LIBERTY HEAD NICKEL

Steeped in mystery when its existence was first revealed, the 1913 Liberty Head nickel is today one of the most famous of U.S. coins. Only five genuine specimens are known to exist. However, numerous alterations have been produced by altering the date of a 1903, 1910, 1912, or other Liberty Head nickel.

Besides its believed surreptitious production by a Mint employee, who later promoted its existence and then tried to sell his products at the 1920 American Numismatic Association convention, the 1913 Liberty Head nickel received further notoriety when, prior to World War II, Texas dealer B. Max Mehl offered to purchase for $50 any specimen discovered. Mehl's gimmick helped promote the sale of his coin catalog, but did not produce any additional examples.

One specimen, now residing in the American Numismatic Association's collection as a donation by Aubrey and Adeline Bebee, is well known for having been the example Wisconsin coin dealer J.V. McDermott regularly carried in his pocket, displayed at bars and gave out on loan to coin clubs.

1918/7-D BUFFALO NICKEL

One of the most famous and dramatic overdates on 20th century U.S. coinage is the 1918/7-D Buffalo nickel. The clearly visible overdate was created when a 1917-dated die was inadvertently struck with a hub for the 1918 coinage. Only a single die is known to have been used. Even in the lowest grades, this rarity brings a high premium. Spurious examples created from normal 1917 or 1918 Denver nickels do exist.

THREE-LEGGED 1937-D BUFFALO NICKEL

Three-legged variety

Normal four-legged nickel

A popular addition to any collection of Buffalo nickels is the 1937-D three-legged variety. This famous variety, which carries high premiums even in low grades, was caused by excessive grinding on the die to remove clash marks. The result was the removal of the lower portion of the bison's front foreleg. The dies used to strike this variety were well-worn, making for a ragged appearance on the Indian's chin and the bison's hind leg and back.

Normal 1937-D nickels that have been altered to pass for the three-legged variety exist, and collectors should be wary. One helpful tip to distinguish the Mint-created 1937-D three-legged nickel from an altered four-legged 1937-D is the positioning of the "P" and "U" in "E Pluribus Unum" in relation to the bison's back. There is additional distance between these two letters and the bison's back on the 1937-D three-legged nickel as compared to the normal four-legged 1937-D.

1939 DOUBLED-DIE JEFFERSON NICKEL

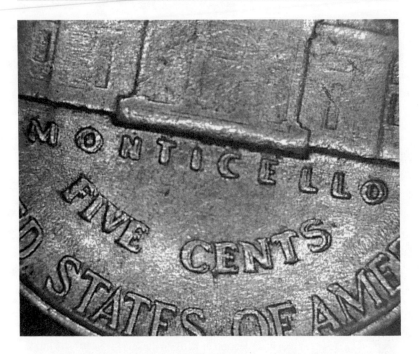

In 1938, the Mint changed from the Buffalo nickel design by James Earle Fraser to the Jefferson nickel design by Felix Schlag. A year later, it produced a major doubled-die coin popular with collectors. The 1939 doubled-die Jefferson nickel displays prominent doubling to the legends "Monticello" and "Five Cents" on the coin's reverse.

1943/2 JEFFERSON NICKEL

Discovered by Del Romines, the 1943/2 Jefferson nickel continues to cause some confusion. There are also some nickels with a die line that can be mistaken for an example of this overdate. On the overdate coin shown here, note the remainder of the numeral "2" following along the line of the bottom curl of the "3." Variety expert Alan Herbert observes that the left base of the "2" protrudes below the "3" and can be seen even on low-grade specimens of this overdate.

HENNING'S COUNTERFEIT NICKEL

One of the most famous counterfeits of the 20th century was produced by Francis Leroy Henning during the early 1950s. Noted for being oversized, overweight, of poor quality and color and sporting a defect in the "R" of "Pluribus," Henning's 1944-dated nickels bore an even more glaring error. Henning failed to observe that genuine wartime silver nickels (1942-1945) displayed a mintmark above the dome of Monticello. Henning, who turned to producing other non-silver dates as well before being arrested in 1955, was eventually sentenced to six years in jail and fined $5,000.

ALTERED 1950-D JEFFERSON NICKEL

In the 1950s and the 1960s, when roll collecting was a craze, the 1950-D was promoted as a rare coin and had a much higher value. Although this is no longer the case, the 1950-D was subject to the creation of specimens made by altering other dates. This example was made by changing the "9" on a 1959-D Jefferson into a "0."

1894-S DIME

The 1894-S dime is undeniably one of the most famous rarities in the U.S. coinage series. Only about a dozen of the original mintage of 24 are believed to exist. As with most rarities, altered examples exist. Many were produced by adding an "S" mintmark to an 1894 dime or by altering an 1894-O. The known genuine specimens display minute die chips at the base and top of the "E" in "Dime."

1942/1 MERCURY DIME

One of the most dramatic overdates of the 20th century, the 1942/1 Mercury dime was not discovered until a year after its release, thus accounting for the number of worn specimens available today. Be particularly careful purchasing specimens of this overdate because numerous forgeries exist (image at right). Some helpful characteristics displayed by genuine examples (see image at top) include the doubling of the numeral "4," a tiny spur connected to the number "9," shooting off toward the top of the "4," and die scratches below the "4." Also note that the numeral "1" appears to the left of the "2" and is slightly lower on genuine examples.

Altered date

1942/1 MERCURY DIME

One helpful tip in determining the authenticity of a 1942/1 Mercury dime is the positioning of the "R" in the word "Liberty" in relation to the wing. Mercury dimes dated 1941 and before show the right leg of the "R" touching the wing. On Mercury dimes from 1942 through 1945, it does not touch. Coins altered from a 1942 to a 1942/1 will show a space at this point.

1876-CC 20-CENT PIECE

The 1876-CC 20-cent piece is by far the greatest rarity in this short-lived coinage series. The termination of the half dime by the Coinage Act of 1873 and a shortage of minor coinage in the West led Senator John Percival Jones to introduce a bill calling for a 20-cent coin in 1874. The new denomination was expected to alleviate problems with daily transactions.

Because of its similarity in size to the quarter dollar, the 20-cent piece was immediately rejected by the public and was only coined for circulation in 1875 and 1876. In 1877, at the order of Mint Director Henry R. Linderman, the remaining Carson City 20-cent pieces were melted. The 1876-CC was a casualty of the melt. Of the original mintage of 10,000 coins, less than two dozen are thought to exist. All genuine specimens show distinct doubling on the word "Liberty" appearing on Liberty's shield.

TYPE I AND TYPE II
STANDING LIBERTY QUARTERS

When sculptor Hermon MacNeil's design for the quarter appeared on the coins of 1916, the first specimens showed a full-length figure of Liberty with an exposed right breast. This Type I modeling for Liberty appeared on the issue dated 1916 and the early strikings of 1917. In 1917, a Type II modeling of Liberty was substituted at MacNeil's request. On subsequent coins, Liberty wears a chain-mail garment over the upper portion of her body.

STANDING LIBERTY QUARTER
DRAPERY FOLD

1916 Type I   1916 Type II

One method of avoiding altered coins is to know the diagnostics of genuine coins. On the 1916 Type I quarter, the lower fold of Liberty's gown is slightly rounded and almost flat across the bottom. This same drapery fold is oval-shaped on the 1917 Type I quarter. This diagnostic is helpful in detecting a 1916-dated quarter created by altering the "7" to a "6" on a 1917 Philadelphia Type I coin. The 1916 Type I quarter carries significant premiums in all grades over its 1917 Type I counterpart.

STANDING LIBERTY QUARTER REVERSE

Type I

Type II

Though most attention focused on the modifications to Liberty's dress on the Type II 1917 Standing Liberty quarter, the reverse also exhibited some changes. Designer Hermon A. MacNeil had complained to Mint Director F.J.H. von Engelken that on the first coins released, the eagle had been dropped too low. This made it look, when soiled, like the tail was connected to the lettering below. MacNeil suggested that the Mint may have made the change to prevent the eagle's right wing from touching the "A" in "America," a feature he liked and which would return to the modified design. He also complained that lowering the eagle gave the appearance of a low-flying or just-rising eagle, and that from his study of the bird, the eagle's talons only extended behind when the eagle is flying at a high altitude. As it appeared on the Type II coins, the eagle was raised and the lettering was re-spaced with three of the 13 stars placed below the eagle.

1921 STANDING LIBERTY QUARTER

The 1921 Standing Liberty quarter carries a significant premium even in lower grades, making it subject to alteration. A popular tool for this purpose has been the lower valued 1924 Standing Liberty quarter, changing the "4" to a "1" to create a coin that could be passed off as an original 1921 quarter. Close examination should reveal such alteration, but another tip is to take note of the style of the first "1" in the date of the 1921 and 1924 coin. The "1" on the 1921 quarter is thicker than that of the 1924 quarter.

1923-S STANDING LIBERTY QUARTER

The 1923-S is one of the key dates in the Standing Liberty quarter series and commands a hefty premium even in lower grades. The chance to make something out of nothing often leads to alteration of less valuable dates in the hope of deceiving unsuspecting collectors. One of the more common forms of deception is the alteration of the "8" on a 1928-S quarter to a "3." This alteration is easily identified. In 1925, the design of the Standing Liberty quarter was changed to show the date area in recess to protect it from wear. Coins altered from a 1928-S quarter will show the date in recess, whereas, an original 1923-S displays a raised date. On a genuine 1923-S, the top of the "3" in the date is flat. The top of the "3" is rounded if the coin has been altered from a 1928-S.

STANDING LIBERTY QUARTER
RECESSED DATE

First released in 1916, it took nine years before the Mint changed the positioning of the date on the Standing Liberty quarter. It was an attempt to stop circulation wear, which led to large numbers of dateless Standing Liberty quarters. In 1925, the design was modified, removing the date from the raised panel and placing it in recess to protect it from circulation wear. The series continued with the recessed date through 1930. (Top image: recessed date; bottom image: wear on a 1920 quarter with date on raised panel.)

JOHN REICH'S 'SCALLOP'

A notch in the 13th star on the lower right of Capped Bust half dollars dating from 1807 through 1815 was apparently the work of John Reich. The Mint engraver from 1807 to 1817, Reich's notch also appeared on the 1808 quarter eagles and certain half eagles. Reich, who was also criticized for using his "fat mistress" on his Capped Bust design, marked his obverse dies with a notch on one of the points of the 13th star.

The notches' existence was noted by M.L. Biestle in 1929. Stewart P. Witham, in an article titled "John Reich's 'Scallops,'" in the November 1967 *Numismatic Scrapbook Magazine*, further linked the mark directly to Reich, observing that the scallop appeared only on Reich's designs and disappeared after Reich left Mint employ in 1817.

1839 'NO DRAPERY'
SEATED LIBERTY HALF DOLLAR

'No Drapery'

Drapery

In 1839, Christian Gobrecht's Seated Liberty design was adopted for the half dollar. The design first appeared on the silver dollars of 1836, the quarters of 1837 and the dimes of 1838. After the Mint had already begun to produce "no drapery" half dollars, a die modification in early 1839 resulted in the addition of an extra fold of drapery extending from Liberty's left elbow to her knee. The "no drapery" 1839 half dollars were released into circulation prior to the change.

WALKING LIBERTY
HALF DOLLAR MINTMARK

Most collectors are familiar with the change in the mintmark positions made early in the coinage of the Walking Liberty half dollar. What is less known is the reason behind the change. When Adolph Weinman's Walking Liberty half dollar was first introduced in 1916, it sported a mintmark just below "In God We Trust" on the obverse of coins struck in Denver and San Francisco.

After beginning branch-mint coinage of the 1917 half dollars with the obverse mintmark, the Mint ordered that the mintmark be moved to the coin's reverse. Mint records show that the change was ordered by Mint Director F.J.H. von Engelken on Feb. 14, 1917. The text of letters held by the Mint, and supplied to *Numismatic News* in 1987, suggest that Von Engelken objected to positioning of the mintmark on the coin's obverse simply because he thought it gave the appearance of a die defect and was too prominent.

The mintmark would remain on the coin's reverse through the end of the series in 1947. The removal of the mintmark during the early part of 1917 created two collectible varieties of that year, with lower mintage on 1917-D and 1917-S coins with the obverse mintmark.

1804 DRAPED BUST SILVER DOLLAR

Class III

Class I

The real story behind the "king of American coins," the 1804 Draped Bust silver dollar, is familiar to most through the 1963 work, *The Fantastic 1804 Dollar,* by Eric P. Newman and Kenneth E. Bressett.

Two 1804 silver dollars, of the 15 specimens known, were struck in 1834 as diplomatic gifts for the king of Siam and the sultan of Muscat. Specimens were also surreptitiously struck at the Mint in the 1850s and 1860s. Bressett and Newman broke the specimens down into three classes based on die positioning and other strike characteristics.

The Class I specimens, of which eight examples are known, can be distinguished from the Class II and Class III dollars by the position of "States Of" in "United States of America" in relation to the clouds on the reverse. For example, the Class I specimens show the "E" in "States" positioned primarily above the fourth cloud from the right. On the Class II (one known) and the Class III specimens, the "E" is between the fourth and fifth clouds from the right. The Class II specimen, struck over an 1857 Swiss shooting taler, is the only specimen with a plain edge.

GOBRECHT DOLLAR

Original

Restrike

During the late 1850s, the Mint's penchant for accommodating coin collectors led to the creation of restrikes of the 1836 through 1839 Gobrecht dollars. The easiest method of distinguishing an original Gobrecht dollar (struck from 1836 through 1839) from one of the restrikes is the die alignment. Though some original Gobrecht dollars used "coin alignment" (reverse inverted when turned) and others "medal alignment" (reverse upright when turned), all show the eagle on the coin's reverse flying upward. The restrikes, however, show the eagle in level flight.

1870-S SEATED LIBERTY SILVER DOLLAR

The 1870-S silver dollar is a classic rarity of the U.S. coinage series. Less than one dozen specimens are thought to exist, with one believed to be in the cornerstone of the San Francisco Mint building. It has been suggested that the limited mintage may have been created for presentation purposes to mark the laying of the cornerstone of the San Francisco Mint building at Fifth and Mission streets. Known examples bear a small, thin "S" mintmark, located close to the eagle, which is uncharacteristic for the period.

CHOP MARKS

The practice of adding "chop marks," or a stamped insignia, to circulating silver coins can be traced to the 18th century. It developed among Oriental merchants as a means of guaranteeing the silver content of coins paid out. Each firm had its own marking and often, after heavy circulation, the design of the host coins would become completely obliterated by chop marks. U.S. Trade dollars, produced from 1873 through 1878 for trade with the Orient sometimes carry chop marks. The chops indicate that some coins did indeed circulate in the Far East, despite the consensus that the Trade dollar was largely a failure for the United States.

1878 MORGAN DOLLAR

Seven tail feathers   *Original eight tail feathers*

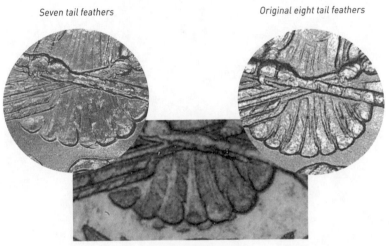

7/8 tail feathers

Shortly after the release of the first Morgan dollar in 1878, new hubs and dies were created. This was ostensibly to lower relief, thereby extending die life, and to correct some minor stylistic concerns.

One stylistic change concerned the proper number of feathers on the eagle's tail. Previous designs featuring an eagle displayed an odd number of tail feathers. The first 1878 examples show an eagle with eight tail feathers. This was deemed inappropriate, and later strikes show only seven tail feathers. Hubs bearing the seven-tail feather design were used to overstrike working dies already struck by an eight-tail feather hub. The result was the popular 1878 7/8 tail feather Morgan dollar variety.

A letter from designer George Morgan to Mint Director Henry R. Linderman, published in the *Comprehensive Catalog and Encyclopedia of U.S. Morgan and Peace Dollars* reveals that 50 dies were overstruck with the new hub. Coins displaying as few as three to as many as seven of the original eight feathers from beneath the new seven-feather design have been identified.

1893-S MORGAN DOLLAR

Despite a mintage of 100,000, the 1893-S Morgan dollar is a great rarity and therefore subject to counterfeiting and alterations. There are a number of things to check in determining a genuine specimen, including a die scratch running across the "T" in "Liberty," as shown in this image. Also check the base of the lower left foot of the "R" (not shown) for two small die marks. In the date, the "1" will be centered directly over a denticle as it is in the second image. As the 1893-S Morgan suffers from altered date and added mintmark specimens, authentication is recommended.

FIRST D-MINT MORGAN DOLLAR

In 1989, an Illinois collector discovered that his bingo change included the fourth 1921-D Morgan dollar released from the first 100 struck by the Denver Mint. It was engraved "4th Dollar Released From 1st 100/Ever Coined At Denver Mint/Thomas Annear Supt." Other examples are known with other numbers, though it is doubtful that all of the first 100 coined were so engraved.

1964 PEACE DOLLAR

A clever mock-up is responsible for the 1964-dated Peace dollar shown above, although the Denver Mint did strike 316,076 coins of that date. The mintage of 45 million silver dollars bearing Anthony De Francisci's design for the 1921-1935 Peace dollar was authorized in August 1964. Production began the following May, but was soon halted. After critics claimed it would benefit only special-interest groups and do little to relieve the coinage shortage, the Treasury recalled and melted existing specimens. If a specimen or specimens did escape the Mint, as is sometimes rumored, the coin or coins have yet to surface and would likely be subject to confiscation by the government.

1776-1976 BICENTENNIAL DOLLAR

Type I

Type II

Shortly after the introduction of the Bicentennial dollar, modifications were made to the obverse and reverse designs, resulting in the creation of two collectible varieties. The relief on the coin's obverse portrait of Dwight D. Eisenhower was lowered to allow better metal flow. Details on the Liberty Bell and moon on the coin's reverse were strengthened, while the lettering in "United States of America" and "One Dollar" was narrowed to conform to the obverse lettering.

The reverse of the Type I Bicentennial dollar, therefore, displays thicker letters and a tail on the final "S" in "States" that extends up to the middle crossbar of the adjacent "E." The Type II specimen has narrow lettering and the tail on the final "S" in "States" extending only slightly above the base of the "E."

NEAR- AND FAR-DATE
1979 ANTHONY DOLLARS

Note the distance between the lines drawn along the base of the dates on these two coin images and the V-shaped start of the coin's rim. The far date is at top; the near date is below.

The 1979 Anthony dollar is known in near-date and far-date varieties. The first strikes from Philadelphia, and those minted in Denver and San Francisco, show the date farther from the rim. Later that year, Philadelphia switched to a die with the date nearer the rim, creating the so-called "near date" 1979 Anthony dollar. According to variety specialist Alan Herbert, although some writers cite the width of the rim as a means of distinguishing the near- from the far-date varieties, both varieties are known to come with either a narrow or a wide rim. The key factor is the distance of the date from the rim.

1849 GOLD DOLLAR
'OPEN/CLOSED WREATH'

Open wreath

Closed wreath

Shortly after the introduction of the nation's first gold dollar in 1849, several modifications were made to James B. Longacre's Type 1 design. The most obvious change was the closing of the wreath on the coin's reverse. The Philadelphia Mint and the Charlotte Mint issues come in both "open wreath" and "closed wreath" varieties. The 1849-C "open wreath" dollar is a great rarity. The Dahlonega and New Orleans issues were the earlier "open wreath" variety only. Variations also exist in the size of the portrait of Liberty on the obverse and the presence or absence of the initial "L" for "Longacre."

1848 'CAL.' QUARTER EAGLE

Sometimes called the first U.S. commemorative coin, the 1848 quarter eagle with "Cal." stamped on the reverse bears a direct link to the California gold rush. In January 1848, James Marshall discovered gold along a sawmill belonging to his employer, Johann Augustus Sutter. Despite attempts to keep the discovery a secret, news of California's newfound wealth traveled quickly. In August, California's military governor, Col. Richard B. Mason, dispatched Lt. Lucien Loeser to Washington, D.C., with samples of California gold. Loeser's samples were subsequently assayed at the Philadelphia Mint, where the gold was transformed into an estimated 1,389 quarter eagles. Each bore a special "Cal." stamp above the eagle as a means of providing special recognition to the source of the gold. Only 50 to 100 of the 1848 "Cal." quarter eagles are thought to remain, many heavily worn.

1911-D INDIAN HEAD QUARTER EAGLE

The 1911-D is the key date in the Indian Head quarter eagle series with a mintage of 55,680. As such, the coin is subject to counterfeiting and authentication is recommended.

Genuine specimens will display a weak mintmark, located to the viewer's left of the fasces on the coin's reverse. High-grade specimens also show a wire rim on the obverse between 12 o'clock and 3 o'clock.

1870-S GOLD $3

Like other 1870 San Francisco Mint coins apparently minted for placement in the new mint's cornerstone, the only specimen known of the 1870-S gold $3 may have been the coin intended for entombment, or it could be a second example. The cornerstone of the Granite Lady, as the mint building came to be known, has not yet been located despite contemporary newspaper accounts of its laying and documentation of much of its contents.

1873 'CLOSED/OPEN 3'

Open 3

Closed 3

Among the more famous coinage varieties are the 1873 "closed 3" and "open 3." Following the U.S. Mint's preparation and initial use of the coinage dies bearing the 1873 date, chief coiner A. Loudon Snowden complained that the "3" in the date appeared more like an "8." To correct the problem, a new logotype showing an open "3" was introduced on all denominations except the half dime, silver dollar, Trade dollar and gold eagle. In the process, several rarities were created, including the proof 1873 $3 gold piece, which comes in "closed-3" and "open-3" varieties.

1804 CAPPED BUST GOLD EAGLE

Plain 4

Crosslet 4

One of the more famous U.S. gold rarities is the 1804 proof eagle with "plain 4" in the date. Despite its 1804 date, this coin was actually struck in 1834 for inclusion in diplomatic presentation cases. Though designated as a restrike by J. Hewitt Judd in his *United States Pattern, Experimental and Trial Pieces*, the 1804 "plain 4" coins were struck from new dies made specifically for these sets' creation.

The 1804 "plain 4" coins also have a beaded border instead of the denticled border found on the 1804 "crosslet 4" originals. Less than a half dozen examples of the 1804 "plain 4" are known to exist.

LARGE- AND SMALL-LETTERS
1839 EAGLE

Type I

Type II

Redesign of Liberty's head in 1839 led to the creation of the so-called large-letters and small-letters 1839 Coronet gold eagle. The Type I 1839 large-letters eagle is a carryover of the design from 1838. During 1839, Christian Gobrecht remodeled the Liberty motif for the coin's obverse. The resulting 1839 Type II design showed smaller lettering on the reverse. The large- and small-letter types can be easily distinguished by viewing the coin's obverse. On the Type I 1839 "Head of 1838" coins, the point of Liberty's coronet is below the sixth star from the viewer's left. On the Type II coins, the coronet point lies more in the center of the space between the sixth and seventh stars and the date appears centered below the figure of Liberty.

1861 PAQUET REVERSE DOUBLE EAGLE

Normal reverse

Paquet reverse

In 1861, Anthony C. Paquet, assistant engraver at the Philadelphia Mint, modified the double eagle's reverse. The most noticeable difference was his use of taller, thinner letters. It was quickly discovered that the new reverse design was wider than the unmodified obverse. The reverse border had become too narrow and would subject the coin to unwanted abrasion. Though the design flaw was discovered quickly, the San Francisco Mint began striking coins with the modified reverse before a message halting coinage arrived from Mint Director James Ross Snowden. Mint records indicate that 19,250 Paquet-reverse double eagles were struck in San Francisco, though less than a dozen examples are known to exist. Less than a half dozen of the Philadelphia Mint Paquet-reverse double eagles are thought to have survived.

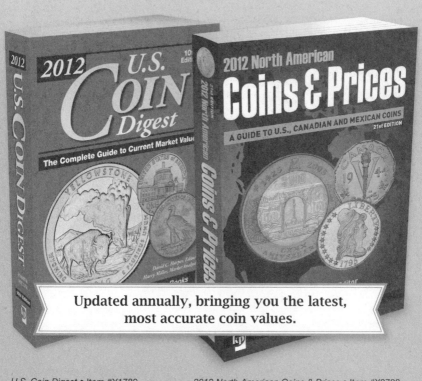